BORING
CAR TRIVIA

3

Written by Richard Porter

Effort has been made to ensure the information in this book is accurate and honest but, as always, mistakes happen. If you're going to write in to complain, please remember to start your message with the words, "I could not contain my surprise and disappointment when I read..."

ISBN: 9798750679676

sniffpetrol.com

CONTENTS

INTRODUCTION

When I wrote the first Boring Car Trivia book in 2020 I had just enough residual boringness to complete a sequel, after which I thought the well was dry. After all, how much arcane information about cars could there be in the world? Enough for two books and no more, I thought, and moved on with my incredibly uninteresting life. But then every so often a new and fantastically dull fact would leap from an article or someone would get in touch on social media and casually mention something absurdly obscure about, oh I don't know, the Citroën CX and like a deeply tedious magpie, I would seize upon it, jotting it down in safe place until suddenly, and to my great surprise, that safe place was bulging was mundane facts, enough for about half a book. The die was cast, and after many months of rooting around there was enough material for this, the third Boring Car Trivia book. If the last two books had a failing, aside from their absurd tiresomeness, it would be that sometimes the entries were rather brief so for this one I've tried to include some longer snippets and stories. In fact, the whole book is longer than either of the previous efforts, though almost certainly no more interesting. I hope you enjoy it because after this there are surely no more boring facts to be unearthed. Or are there…?

Richard Porter, Sniff Petrol
October 2021

5

FOREWORD
by Jonny Smith

Apparently Richard Hammond was supposed to write this foreword, but he was too busy dredging his moat. If he had, I suspect Hammond would have used more exclamation marks than me, and mentioned that he and Porter share a love for Land Rovers. One Life Live It, Brit icon etc. If you're reading someone else's copy of this book please buy your own so that Richard (Porter) can afford a house with a garage. Knowing he street parks his Defender stresses me out immensely. Rugged they may be, but they rust alarmingly quickly for a car proudly made from aluminium.

I didn't grow up knowing Richard, but I am certain he was one of those lads who knew the registration numbers of his mate's parent's cars. And the dealer name sticker in the back window. Like 'Dennis Toejam Vauxhall of Daventry' in a faintly jazzy font. Richard would also be acutely aware of the spec of said cars (and the list price of said options), the elaborate name given to the paint hue by the manufacturer, and also where these cars ranked in his neural Filofax.

Was Jed's Mum's Alfasud better than Dominic's Dad's Carlton Diplomat saloon? Why did Hannah's mum's Fiesta have such a stupidly high idle speed? Why did Ian's uncle have aftermarket hubcaps on his Escort Ghia? It makes it look so...so... disappointing.

So many questions - important questions to the mind of a future car book author.

Richard didn't come from a family of exotic car owners. He (like me) was surrounded by charmless cars, which actually made them strangely memorable. If his Dad had taken him and his brother to cub scouts in a Maserati Biturbo I honestly don't think that his automotive encyclopaedia would have ended up being so nutritiously packed with vehicle facts. Travelling around in charmless cars possibly acted as the perfect catalyst (you remember seeing those badges on the boots of '80s Volvos, no?) for knowing all about boring vehicles. Besides, every Tom, Dick and Tossface knows how fast a Porsche 959 was, or that Rowan Atkinson crashed his McLaren F1 several times. But the sign of a true carficionado is being able to appreciate the shared switch gear between otherwise unrelated machines. Or the true story for the parts bin share. Facts cannot be debated, whereas subjective comments like 'all people who bought Bedford CF vans probably murdered a relative' can. And should.

Don't tell him, but I am incredibly proud of Porter's boring car trivia. Because it is never boring. Every downstairs toilet bookshelf was born to bear a volume.

Jonny Smith

WARNING
May causes drowsiness

The latest Dacia Sandero appears to have fashionable state-of-the-art LED rear lights but Dacia's tight cost controls wouldn't run to real LEDs so the lamps are actually old-fashioned bulbs with a mask over the top to give an LED effect.

The mark 3 Granada of 1985 always looked a bit under-wheeled at the back because Ford accountants wouldn't authorise changes to widen the carried-over rear axle from the smaller Sierra leaving the wheels looking too inboard and 'lost' within the arches. A similar problem afflicted the Talbot Tagora because PSA took over during the car's development, insisted on greater parts sharing with its own cars to save money, and imposed upon it the rear axle from the narrower Peugeot 505.

Possible names for the original VW Polo included Bonito, Euros, Pony, and Mini-Golf.

In Europe the Renault Fuego died in the mid-eighties, but it was on sale in Argentina until 1992. The last Fuego was made in France in June 1985 but the Argentinian factory was just getting into its stride at that point, churning out the same model for another seven years and even treating it to a facelift in 1988, at which point the unusual ribbed plastic side strip was made smooth and body coloured and the car was renamed the Fuego GTA.

The Citroën CX was designed to accept a range of engines including a flat four, an air-cooled flat six, and a Wankel rotary motor. In the end not one of these made it to production.

You might assume Honda's involvement in the third generation Rover 200, codenamed R3, extended only as far as authorising the use of the chassis from the Anglo-Japanese mk2 200/Concerto (albeit cut down and fitted with the torsion beam rear axle from the Maestro/Montego). In fact, early in the car's genesis some of its bodyshell engineering was assisted by Honda engineers on secondment to the UK, working on specially imported Japanese-spec CAD stations installed within Rover's Canley design centre. Then, later in the development process, Honda realised they could do with a smaller car to sit below the Civic in European showrooms and asked if they might come to some agreement to re-badge the R3. The plan was given the codename R3-H and sketches were created to show how a cost-effective re-badging job might look. The idea was nixed when BMW bought Rover in January 1994 and the R3 went on sale in 1995 exclusively as a Rover.

The Ford Racing Puma was never a model in its own right, thereby ducking the need to go through full homologation. Officially speaking, each Racing Puma was simply a Ford Puma 1.7 with the optional Racing Puma pack. If so ordered, a lightly modified Puma 1.7 came off the Cologne production line minus its bumpers and sitting on basic steel wheels. It was then shipped to Tickford in Daventry where the bespoke Racing parts including wider wings, new bumpers and MIM Speedline alloy wheels were fitted. Tickford originally offered anyone who had ordered the 'Racing Puma pack' the chance to visit the factory to watch their car in the midst of conversion but this was quickly found to be disruptive and the offer was withdrawn.

In 1981 Pontiac turned down a request from a TV company for three identical Trans Ams for a new series about a talking car because the company's sales promotion manager thought the show 'sounded silly'. However, Pontiac's West Coast PR man, having successfully placed a Trans Am in Smokey and the Bandit and a Firebird in The Rockford Files, saw potential in the idea and got backing from other members of Pontiac management in order to win over the reluctant sales promotion manager and secure the cars the TV producers wanted. Knight Rider went on to become a big success, lasting for 84 episodes over a four-year run.

Tuesday 4 May 1999 was an important landmark in the development of the Volvo XC90. That was the day when three design proposals – one from the main studio in Gothenburg, two from the Volvo Monitoring and Concept Center in California – were brought together in one place so that senior management could pick a favourite to be taken through to production. The location for this shootout was Volvo's proving ground in Wittmann, Arizona where the three full-size styling models were arranged on the tarmac so they could be assessed at leisure in a secure outdoor location. Naturally, the bosses wanted to take their time over such a big decision, what with this being the company's first effort in the fashionable SUV market. However, their deliberation caused some consternation for design boss Peter Horbury and his team because in the 41 degree heat of the Arizona desert the clay models were starting to melt.

In 2002 the Queen was presented with a brand-new Bentley State Limousine. It's rarely said that she actually received two identical examples, just in case.

Amount of welding in a standard Metro bodyshell:

4 feet

Amount of welding in a Metro 6R4 bodyshell:

137 feet

CODENAMES USED BY FORD OF EUROPE IN THE 1970s

Diana – mark 2 Capri named after secretary working on project (launched 1974)
Brenda – mark 2 Escort (1975)
Linda - aborted mark 4 Cortina replacement (1976-77)
Eva – mark 2 Granada (1977)
Carla - mark 3 Capri (1978)
Teresa - Cortina 80 (1979)
Erika - mark 3 Escort (1980)
Gloria – mark 2 Granada facelift (1982)
Toni – Sierra (1982)

In January 2004 MG Rover simultaneously launched facelifts for its 25, 45 and 75 ranges but the impact of this was somewhat reduced because the company accidentally released newspaper adverts in the Daily Mirror and the London Evening Standard which showed off these new models three days before their official announcement.

Steven Spielberg got permission to film scenes for 1989's Indiana Jones and the Last Crusade around the Khazneh temple in Petra after meeting King Hussein of Jordan at a shooting party organised by tartan clothing enthusiast Jackie Stewart.

The population of Arjeplog in Northern Sweden more than doubles in winter months, entirely thanks to the car engineers who descend on the area to perform cold weather testing. About 1900 people normally live in the town while at peak testing time the population exceeds 4000. All told, the car industry is reckoned to put an annual $170m into the local economy.

Between 1991 and 1998 the Renault Clio was advertised on UK television using two French characters, Papa and Nicole. During all this time actor Max Douchin who played Papa uttered just three different words on screen; 'Nicole', 'Maman' and 'Bernard', while Estelle Skornik who played Nicole said only two; 'Papa' and 'Bob'.

The village of Hethel in Norfolk is not just famous as the home of Lotus. It's also noted for containing what's believed to be the UK's oldest living hawthorn tree, reputed to be more than 700 years old and to be found in the village churchyard.

In 1991 Rover and Honda signed a memorandum of understanding to formalise future cooperation. Out of this came plans for a range of jointly developed cars, each given an 'SK' codename. The first product of this new plan was SK1, launched in 1993 as the Rover 600. SK2 was the code for later, Rover-engined versions of the same car. SK3 was a small car that evolved into the R3 Rover 200 and SK4 became the 1995 Rover 400. SK5, a replacement for the Rover 800, never saw light of day. The SK codename came from the surnames of the Rover and Honda bosses at the time, George Simpson and Nobuhiko Kawamoto.

The doors on the Citroën XM estate were the ones from the hatchback with plastic cappings bonded to their tops to match the higher roofline. The estates were built by Heuliez using part-completed XM hatchbacks which were shipped over from Citroën to have their bespoke rear ends fitted.

The fourth-generation Nissan Micra of 2010 featured two unusual 'ripple' marks on its roof, supposedly inspired by a stone being dropped into a pond. A more accurate, if less romantic reason was that the 'ripples' added strength to the roof panel which meant that the metal used for the pressing could be thinner and therefore cheaper and lighter.

The SAAB 99 of 1968 was codenamed Project Gudmund because development officially started on 2 April 1964 and in Sweden the second of April is the name day for people called Gudmund.

The Morris Minor was the first British car to sell one million units.

In November 2020 Toyota of Australia issued a recall for the Hilux pick-up because of a missing sticker. All vehicles sold in Australia are supposed to come with a compliance label showing that they meet Australian Design Rules on safety and emissions but on the Hiluxes in question this sticker was missing. According to Toyota's official recall notice, owners of the affected pick-ups were asked to take their trucks to their nearest dealer where the sticker would be attached in a process that would take "approximately 30 minutes". The number of Hiluxes affected by this very serious recall was 15.

Although the Aston Martin DB7 used many parts from the Ford empire of the time, including Mazda rear lights and door handles, its side repeaters were made by Hella and also found on various Volkswagens including the Golf mk2 and Corrado.

Crewe local council has an unofficial agreement with Bentley not to re-surface a bumpy road near the car maker's factory because its bad surface is a great test of ride quality and forms part of an in-house 'evaluation loop' which senior management people drive to sign off new chassis settings.

Brutal honesty is not something you expect from car company representatives launching a new product. But at the 2015 first drive event for the facelifted MG6 product manager Andrew Lowerson told the assembled press, "when you sit in the MG6, it won't be as good as a Škoda Octavia. But it's £7000 cheaper than the equivalent Škoda Octavia".

To make it easier to heel-and-toe the GR Yaris, Toyota engineers enlarged the accelerator pedal by 5mm.

Since the 1970s Renault had been toying with making a small, cheap, functional car to sit below the R5 and act as a spiritual replacement for the Renault 4. Unfortunately, the numbers didn't make economic sense and in 1985, with the company losing money all over the place, bosses cancelled their latest plans for a cheaper car. This prompted a rather unusual response from the Confédération Générale du Travail trade union which decided to design its own low-cost Renault, partly as a commitment to the egalitarian idea of affordable transport for the masses and partly because they hoped it could be built in Renault's Billancourt factory, averting its closure and the resultant mass redundancies. Their design, very boxy and basic with overtones of the Renault 4, was labelled the Neutral (an anagram of Renault) and presented to management as a full-size mock-up in November 1986. Unfortunately for La CGT, Renault chairman Georges Besse and his team were not sold on the union's plan and gave it a flat 'non'. Just 10 days later Besse was assassinated for unrelated reasons. Besse's successor, Raymond Lévy, decided to re-focus Renault's efforts in Europe, bringing the idea of the cheaper car back into play. Rather than re-activate the Neutral, however, he ordered work to re-start on another mothballed small car project, codenamed W60, but to avoid alerting the powerful union to the fact their proposal had been ignored in favour of an existing in-house effort, the internal code number was flipped around and the prefix changed from a W (Renault code for a project under consideration) to X (project intended for production). The result was Projet X06 which became the original Twingo.

The first-generation RenaultSport Clio V6 was built in Sweden. The cars were assembled in the AutoNova factory in Uddevalla, a joint venture between TWR and Volvo which also made the Volvo C70. For the second-generation V6, production moved to the RenaultSport plant in Dieppe.

The mk1 Ford Escort RS2000 of 1973 almost wasn't badged the RS2000. The original plan was to call it the Ford Escort Puma.

In the early seventies GM's crash testing department got some unexpected cannon fodder when the company bought back a load of brand-new but water-damaged Buicks from a flooded Pennsylvania dealership. The unsaleable cars were smashed into prototypes of upcoming models as part of their safety testing regime. One model to benefit from this was the massive and none-more-seventies GMC Motorhome.

In the early eighties Ford of Europe stopped using women's names to label new car programmes and adopted characters from Greek mythology. This scheme was swiftly dropped in favour of alpha-numeric codes but the replacement for the Ford Granada, known in its later stages as DE-1, got its old mythological codename back for production and was launched in 1985 as the Ford Scorpio (except in the UK and Ireland where it kept the Granada name and just used Scorpio as the top trim level until 1994).

There are several car models that had uncommonly brief existences but it's rare to find a whole car factory that was remarkably short-lived. Unless, that is, we're talking about the SAAB factory in Malmö which opened in 1989 and closed before it had reached its second birthday in 1991. The plant, established within an old shipyard with encouragement from the Swedish government to offset the disastrous collapse of the nation's shipbuilding industry, was state-of-the-art for the time and assembled SAAB 900s on a team principle rather than with a moving production line. Unfortunately, the cars it made were said to be of inferior quality to those coming from the main plant at Trollhätten and each lost the company a whopping $18,180. Little wonder when GM took over SAAB in 1990 the Malmö factory was quickly singled out for closure and assembled its last car on 30 June 1991.

The Austin-Healey Sprite of 1958 was intended to have flip-forward headlights, as later seen on the Porsche 928. They were fitted to the first prototype but it was then decided that such an arrangement added needless cost and complication to a cheap, simple roadster and thereafter the lamps were fixed in place, giving the car the distinctive look that led to its 'Frogeye' nickname.

When McLaren engineers were developing the Mercedes SLR McLaren they bought a brand new Aston Martin Vanquish in order to do some 'competitor analysis'. The car was stripped down, assessed, and then re-assembled before being sold back to the Surrey dealer that had supplied it. According to one of this dealership's former salesman, it was the best-made second hand Vanquish they ever saw.

RenaultSport is rightly famed for its superb chassis work on cars such as the Clio 172 and Mégane R26.R but the Dieppe-based suspension maestros also had complete responsibility for development of the never-popular Renault Wind convertible.

1100 Special (1979)
25 (1984)
35 (1994)
40 (1999)
Advantage (1987)
British Open Classic (1992)
Checkmate (1990)
Chelsea (1985)
Cooper (1990)*
Cooper 35 (1996)
Cooper Grand Prix (1994)
Cooper Monte Carlo (1994)
Cooper S Touring (1997)
Cooper S Works (1999)
Cooper Sport 500 (2000)
Cooper Sports (1998)
Designer (1988)
Equinox (1996)
ERA Turbo (1990)
Flame (1989)
Flame Red (1990)

BL/AUSTIN ROVER/ROVER MINIS
2000)

Italian Job (1992)
Jet Black (1988)
John Cooper LE 40 (1999)
Mayfair (1982)
Neon (1991)
Park Lane (1987)
Paul Smith (1998)
Piccadilly (1986)
Racing (1988)
Racing Green (1989)
Red Hot (1988)
Rio (1993)
Ritz (1985)
Rose (1989)
Sidewalk (1995)
Sky (1989)
Sprite (1983)**
Studio 2 (1990)
Tahiti (1993)
Thirty (1989)

*Initially a special edition before becoming permanent part of range
**In 1992 Sprite brought back as permanent part of the range, replacing the City as base model.

Many cars boast of being able to fit a golf bag in the boot but in 1995 Holden went one better when it announced a special Greg Norman edition of the Statesman International which came with an actual set of golf clubs as standard. The 250-off limited edition also featured two-tone paint, a sunroof, leather seats, 16-inch alloys, fog lights, woodgrain trim and Greg Norman signature badging. The original run of 250 cars was such a hit that in 1997 they decided to make 300 more.

The Audi factory in Györ, Hungary has the largest rooftop solar panel array in Europe with a photovoltaic area larger than 22 football pitches. 160,000 square metres of panels produce 9.5 GWh of electricity every year which would be enough to run 3800 households if the power wasn't needed to operate the factory which builds the Audi TT, Q3, A3 saloon and cabrio, and almost two million engines a year for use across the entire VAG empire.

Morgan still makes the frames for its rear wheel arches from strips of wood laminate pressed together in a curved jig dating back to the 1950s. When the company adopted - shock! - computer aided design to create its new generation of models it discovered that the curve on the jig wasn't consistent. Rather than go to the trouble and expense of designing a new jig when the old one worked perfectly well, the company simply adjusted the frame curvature in the CAD data so that the digital model was also slightly imperfect.

In 1974 Rover dispatched a prototype of the yet-to-be-announced SD1 to the Stelvio Pass between Italy and Switzerland to conduct brake tests on punishing gradients. As befitted a top-secret model, the prototype was painted completely black and fitted with matt black camouflage panels covering the entire nose and tail, all intended to make the car as unnoticeable as possible. Unfortunately, it turned out to be too unnoticeable and during testing it was crashed into by some German tourists in a Ford Taunus. After that the Rover brake test team decided to compromise the low profile of their lightly dinked prototype with strips of yellow reflective tape across the nose.

In 1981 Chrysler launched a special Frank Sinatra Edition of its Imperial coupé which came with gold plated FS medallions on the sides and rear, a choice of velvet or leather seats, and a leather tote bag containing 16 cassettes of Sinatra albums, though annoyingly the special lockable tape cubby in the centre console had room for only eight cassettes at a time. Just 278 Imperial Frank Sinatra Editions were sold, each painted light blue to match the colour of ol' blue eyes, erm, eyes.

In order to set-up the passive steer characteristics of the 'Weissach' rear axle to be fitted to the 928, Porsche engineers modified an Opel Admiral saloon with a rear-steering system, operated by a wheel in the back seat. This development hack was then repeatedly driven at speed into corners and an engineer in the back would input different levels of steering to work out the amount of deflection that should be allowed by the bushes in the 928's rear axle. The person in the back had to be quick, though. It was reckoned that their inputs needed to be within 0.2 of a second to give an accurate picture of how much a given wheel angle stabilised the high-speed handling.

The original Lotus Elan wouldn't have met rules about minimum headlamp height without pop-up lamps but designer Ron Hickman wanted to avoid the complexity and extra weight of motors to power them. Instead, he proposed a manually operated system which he tested by mounting a headlight rig to the front of Colin Chapman's Jaguar Mark 2 which he then drove up and down the M1 to make sure the lamps could be popped up under the pressures of high speeds. It turned out they could not, and at the last minute the Elan's pop-ups became vacuum operated instead.

From October 1968 onwards MGBs and MG Midgets sold in North America featured a third windscreen wiper. This was to meet updated Federal regulations about the percentage of the screen that had to be covered by the wipers. Over the years other models to have featured three windscreen wipers include the Toyota FJ Cruiser, Toyota Mega Cruiser, UMM Alter, Maserati Quattroporte II, some Jaguar E-types, and various Morgans.

The first mass-produced American car with rack-and-pinion steering was the Ford Pinto, launched in 1970. The second was the AMC Pacer.

Like many car makers, Nissan sometimes confects special editions as a way of shifting units without having to discount existing trim levels. In 2004 it needed a short-notice Micra special to give sales a giddy-up so chucked a load of extras on the S trim grade and then realised there wasn't time to have special badges created before the planned on-sale date. So the marketing people simply took the badge from the upspec SX model, turned it upside down and – hey presto! - the new special edition Nissan Micra XS.

The Subaru Vivio Kei car of the 1990s got its name from converting the individual numbers of its engine capacity, 660cc, into Roman numerals. VI + VI + 0 = VIVIO

For much of the 20th century Citroën's product planning strategy was to make its flagship cars so advanced that they could remain in production for a long time without becoming dated, thereby offsetting the higher development costs of their forward-looking engineering. Hence the Traction Avant lasted from 1934 until 1957, the DS was in production from 1955 until 1975, and the CX lived from 1974 until 1991.

The current Ford GT is made in Canada. Other Canadian-made cars include the Dodge Challenger. Its great rival, the Chevrolet Camaro, was also made there between 2009 and 2015 before production moved to the United States.

The VW Beetle was first exported to the US in 1949. The total number of Beetles sold to Americans that year was... two. Things went rather better after that and by the end of the fifties Americans had to join a six month waiting list to get a Beetle. In 1968, the model's best year in the United States, VW sold 399,674 of 'em.

Although GM took back and crushed most EV1 electric cars in the early 2000s, a fully working example lives on at the company's Tech Center in Warren, Michigan and has a dedicated engineer devoted to its upkeep.

The first Austin/MG Metro with a five-speed gearbox was the 6R4 rally car.

The project which became the 1991 Volvo 850 had many codenames during a protracted development period that began in 1978. One of those codenames, introduced in 1986 and dropped in 1987, was Project S which came about after Volvo decided to stop developing the hatchback version of the car and concentrate on the saloon. The S didn't stand for saloon or sedan though. It was chosen because the hatchback was officially cancelled on the birthday of Queen Silvia of Sweden. Obviously.

The Mercedes-Benz 450 SEL 6.9 could be had with futuristic options such as ABS and a phone, but Q-car enthusiasts might argue the most important request for the order form was option code 261 - badge delete.

When committed vegetarian Sir Paul McCartney bought a Lexus LS600h the car had to be specially ordered with cloth rather than leather seats.

The Range Rover CSK special edition of 1990 was named after Charles Spencer King, the 'godfather' of the original Range Rover. King himself wasn't involved in developing this model, but he was asked to write out his initials over and over again until the designers had an iteration they liked which was turned into the model's identifying decals applied to the sides and bootlid.

Citroën once developed a helicopter. The RE-2 project, started in 1973, was an effort to find a use for the Wankel rotary engine the company had been developing since the 1960s and which it was intending to fit into its cars, specifically the CX, until the oil crisis put such a thirsty motor on the back burner. Helicopter development continued throughout the seventies until Citroën's masters at Peugeot called time on it in 1979. The lone prototype still exists and lives in the Citroën heritage collection.

Renault boss Pierre Dreyfus wanted the R4 of 1961 to be a "jeans car", because jeans were something "which people can wear in any situation if you do away with the pretentions of snobbism and social conformity". By coincidence, in 1980 Giorgetto Giugiaro described the Fiat Panda as "like a pair of jeans: a simple, practical article of clothing without pretence". Neither of these cars should be confused with the Volkswagen Jeans Beetle of 1973 which was literally like a pair of jeans because it had seats made of denim.

Upon its announcement in 1976 the Rover 3500 or SD1 received great praise for its excellent exterior styling, but the low, swooping design and rear-wheel-drive chassis compromised the interior space on this British Leyland flagship. As a result, any BL employee planning to attend the car's press launch at Chateau Impney in Worcestershire in a lesser but more spacious Austin Princess was told to park it well away from the new Rovers to prevent journalists from being able to make an easy and potentially damning comparison between the new executive model and its cheaper relative.

The original Volkswagen Polo was first launched as an Audi. The Audi 50, designed in Ingolstadt with input from Bertone, was announced in August 1974. The Volkswagen version wasn't revealed until March 1975. The Audi 50 was discontinued in July 1978.

The world's first car with sat-nav as standard was the European-market Lexus LS400 of 1998.

Early mules for the fourth generation L405 Range Rover used the understructure of the new model clothed in panels from its predecessor, crudely decorated with tacked-on arch extensions and old Defender front lamps. When their working lives on the L405 project were over, some of these rough-and-ready hacks had a second life as test cars for the L494 Range Rover Sport which was made from the same platform as the L405, enabling Land Rover engineers to perform early development work on two separate model ranges using one set of mules.

At the launch of the strange, two-seater Mini Coupé in 2011, its creators claimed that the car's roof was inspired by a backwards baseball cap.

In 2007 GM announced an exciting-sounding Z0K Club Sport package for the Pontiac Solstice two-seater which, for $1095, brought a limited slip diff, thicker anti-roll bars, re-valved dampers, higher rate springs and a seven millimetre drop in ride height. Unfortunately, this last aspect meant the cars sat too low to negotiate the existing production line and shipping ramps so GM's engineers installed what they referred to as "supplemental second spring seats" within the suspension which temporarily jacked up each Z0K-spec car to avoid snags. So far, so good. But then it all went very GM because the company issued a memo to dealers stating that if the customer wanted these suspension spacers removed for a reason such as, let's say, having paid almost two grand for a handling package and wanting their car to perform as intended, they would have to pay for the pleasure. If they didn't, they would simply drive around with the car at its shipping ride height and the carefully tuned Club Sport chassis being all but pointless.

There is a waterfall inside every Lexus factory. Its purpose is to capture dust and the tiny particles of overspray escaping from the painting process thereby ensuring a better finish on the cars.

When a Belgian F-16 pilot called Rudi Thoelen won the inaugural Land Rover G4 Challenge in 2003 he turned down the first prize of a brand-new Range Rover. Instead he asked for, and was given, two Land Rover Defenders.

When Anakin Skywalker adjusts the controls in his podracer during the 1999 movie Star Wars – The Phantom Menace what he's operating is the wiper control unit from a mk1 Fiat Uno mounted upside-down alongside a generic Austin Rover electric mirror adjuster (as detailed in the first volume of this boring car trivia series).

The official codename of the Renault 4 was Projet 112 but internally it was nicknamed '350' because its target price was 350,000 Francs. The design brief for the car was that it should be more attractive than its intended rival, the Citroën 2 CV, but less desirable than Renault's own larger and more expensive Dauphine.

Early mules for the R40 project which became the Rover 75 were Rover 600s fitted with KV6 engines and entire R40 underparts grafted beneath the shells of Rover 800 Coupés (chosen over the 800 saloon because they had greater body rigidity and were therefore closer to the calculated stiffness of the finished shell). A keen-eyed car nerd could spot these hacks because the 600s had bonnet humps while the 800s wore a fuel filler flap on the British offside where a normal Coupé had its filler on the nearside.

Many of the car stunts in Knight Rider were made possible because of a train derailment. The first series of the show was made with just a handful of Trans Ams, three of them donated by GM, limiting the number of stunts that could be filmed. Fortunately for the show's producers, on 11 November 1982 (the day before episode eight of Knight Rider series one was first transmitted) a train carrying Firebirds and Camaros from GM's assembly plant in Van Nuys, California came off the tracks just south of Fresno and, though many of the cars on board were largely undamaged, under Californian law they could not be sold since technically they had been in an accident. Instead, GM gave 12 of the Firebirds to the producers of Knight Rider for $1 each and they were used on the show thereafter, vastly increasing the number of car-punishing stunts that could be filmed. Many of the other cars from the train accident were used as cannon fodder in The Fall Guy, made by the same production company. GM's only stipulation was that these cars had to be crushed once their on-camera life was over.

In the 2000s Mercedes got it into its corporate head that almost every model it made had to be sent to AMG to have a massive V8 stuffed under the bonnet. The zenith of this thinking was the R 63 L AMG of 2006, a terminally fugly 503 horsepower six-seater that cost £74,000. The R 63 was such a niche idea that it lasted in production for just one year, during which time a mere 12 examples made it to the UK.

Officially, the Fiat Coupé was actually called the Coupé Fiat. The confusingly named car had Pininfarina badges on its sides but only because the design house built the car (and styled its interior). The exterior was by Chris Bangle.

The Range Rover CSK of 1990 was a limited edition of which just 200 were made, each with a numbered plaque on the dashboard stating its place in the build run so that a customer might take satisfaction in having one of the first or last ones off the line. Except this wasn't quite as it seemed because the person responsible for the plaques stacked them the wrong way up so that the first car made was 200/200 and the last came out labelled 001/200. Not that this mattered much at the time because the CSK's slightly weird spec - two-door shell, black paint, silver bumpers, American walnut interior trimmings and, unless you specced otherwise, a manual gearbox - made it a sales disaster. They're quite sought after today though.

The Ferrari 456 uses the same pop-up headlight motors as the Volvo 480. However, the 456 also has another one of these motors in the back bumper where it powers a hidden moveable spoiler.

When it went on sale in 1980 the Fiat Panda came with a choice of two engines. The Panda 30 had the two-cylinder, 652cc engine from the Fiat 126 while the Panda 45 came with the throbbing four-cylinder, 903cc motor from the Fiat 127. From the front you could tell a Panda 30 from a Panda 45 by the asymmetrical stamped metal slots of the grille, those of the 30 sat to the left with the Fiat badge on the right while the 45 flipped this arrangement. This was of no consequence in the UK, because the Panda 30 wasn't sold here, and of no consequence elsewhere after 1984 when all Pandas got a full-width black plastic grille.

When the original Chevrolet Corvette went on sale in 1953 it was available only with a 3.9-litre straight six. A V8 didn't arrive until 1955.

In the 2000s there was an art-punk band from Seattle called Talbot Tagora. According to their official biog they were not named in tribute to the ill-fated saloon car but after a relative's cat which in turn got its name from the never-popular early eighties executive car for reasons that seem lost to the mists of time. Perhaps it was a very boxy cat.

In 2003 Opel announced a special edition version of the Speedster, their Vauxhall VX220, created to celebrate rocktastic whistling enthusiasts The Scorpions. Based on the 197 horsepower Turbo model, the Speedster Scorpions came only in silver with black wheels, blacked-in exterior trim, a chrome Scorpions badge, and a Gibson Flying V guitar signed by all five members of the band so that, according to official Opel bumf at the time, "from now on you can join in without compromise". Just 60 Speedster Scorpions were made.

The 2003 'remake' of The Italian Job featured a scene in which three BMW-era Minis drove into a Los Angeles subway station. The people in charge of the LA Metro system didn't want any fumes in their underground tunnels so the cars used in this sequence were converted by the movie makers to electric power and the internal combustion engine noises were added in post-production.

The 1955 DS was not the first Citroën to be fitted with the company's hydropneumatic suspension. It was pre-dated by the 15/6 H of 1954, a six-cylinder version of the Traction Avant equipped with hydropneumatics on the rear axle.

It has become an established car 'fact' that the first BMW Mini had the same wheelbase as an original Range Rover but this isn't true. The R50 Mini's wheelbase is 97 inches, the classic Range Rover's 100 inches. Only with the introduction of the five-door model in 2014 did the regular Mini get a wheelbase greater than that of a first-generation Range Rover. Cars that do have a 100 inch wheelbase just like a classic Range Rover include the Citroën C3 Picasso, the Ford RS200, the AMC Pacer, the Fiat Coupé, and the Ford Model T.

There have been two cars called EV1. One was GM's electric car of the late 1990s, the Electric Vehicle 1, the other was a SAAB concept car, the EV-1 (with a hyphen) which was a 900 Turbo-based concept car with a cool coupe body and a solar panel roof. In this case the name stood for Experimental Vehicle 1.

Aston Martin was able to make the one-off Victor after discovering it had a prototype carbon fibre tub and a leftover 7.3-litre V12 from the One-77 project in its stores. The tub was re-furbished by Multimatic, the company that originally made it, and the V12 re-built by Cosworth before the car was assembled to the specifications of its buyer, a probably-not-poor Aston Martin fan from Belgium.

In the mid-seventies Citroën toyed with creating a more luxurious 'super Deux Chevaux' with the four-cylinder engine from the GS as well as a retro chrome grille inspired by the Traction Avant, chrome wheels, opening rear windows, a metal panel instead of the roll-back canvas roof, and a spare wheel mounted on the bootlid. A single prototype was built in 1974, labelled the 2 CV Pop, before the idea was abandoned.

HOW LONG IT TOOK CERTAIN
ICONIC MODELS TO REACH THE
ONE MILLION MILESTONE

VAZ-2105 - three years and eight months
(launched April 1970, millionth car made in December 1973)

Renault 4 – Four years and four months*
(launched October 1961, millionth car made in February 1966)

BMC Mini – five years and six months
(launched August 1959, millionth car made in February 1965)

Morris Minor – 12 years and four months
(launched September 1948, millionth car made in January 1961)

Citroën 2 CV - 12 years and five months
(launched October 1948, millionth car made in March 1961)

*Appropriate

CARS THAT LASTED FOR ONLY
ONE GENERATION

Alfa Romeo Brera
Alfa Romeo GT
Alfa Romeo MiTo
Audi A2
Citroën C4 Cactus
Fiat Barchetta
Fiat Coupé
Fiat Idea
Fiat Multipla
Honda CRZ
Honda S2000
Mercedes-Benz CLS Shooting Brake
Mercedes-Benz R-Class
Mini Coupé and Roadster
Mini Paceman
Peugeot RCZ
Renault Avantime
Renault Modus
Renault Vel Satis
Smart Roadster
Suzuki X-90
Vauxhall Signum
Volkswagen Corrado
Volkswagen Eos
Volkswagen Phaeton
Volvo C30

When Renault put the proposed design for the Twingo through customer clinics 75 percent of those polled weren't sure about its looks. In fact, half of those asked really hated it. Design boss Patrick le Quément persuaded management that the 25 percent who loved it so much they wanted to buy one immediately were the people to trust. In a note to Renault chairman Raymond Lévy he wrote, "The greatest risk is not to take any risks, and I ask you to vote for instinctive design against extinctive marketing." Lévy's reply was simple and to the point; "I agree." The Twingo went ahead to the proposed design.

Production of the 991-shape Porsche 911 GT2 RS ended in February 2019 only to re-start a few weeks later. Then, after four cars had been made, it stopped again, this time for good. The brief return can be explained by events of March 2019 when a cargo ship called the Grande America caught fire and sank in the Bay of Biscay. On board were 37 Porsches bound for Brazil, including four examples of the 991 GT2 RS. To keep valued Brazilian customers happy Porsche decided to re-start production to replace the cars lost at sea and the four brand-new GT2s arrived safely in Brazil in June 2019.

In November 1980 Ford launched the XR3 version of its new mk3 Escort by parking 340 Sunburst Red examples on a recently finished and unopened section of the M4 motorway just near the company's new Bridgend plant where the car's CVH engine was made. Another 64 were parked in formation in the factory car park to spell out XR3. The company then bussed in journalists and dealers to drive away in the cars, the new motorway's smooth surface presumably quite flattering to the original XR3's famously terrible ride.

The showroom version of the Toyota GR Yaris has little plastic covers on the underside of the bonnet concealing holes in the panel's inner skin which were put there to give a tiny bit of extra room for the longer travel front struts of the WRC version.

In 1966 Ford decided to present I Got You Babe singing enthusiasts Sonny & Cher with a pair of Mustangs, customised by California-based car fiddler George Barris. Sonny's car was brown and gold, Cher's was pink, and both featured heavily modified front and rear ends, the noses gaining rectangular headlights that made them look a bit like fancy Vauxhall Vivas. Cher's interior was trimmed in white ermine and pink suede, Sonny's in bobcat fur and saddle leather. Obviously. Both cars ran a 4.7-litre V8, though Sonny's had the 225 horsepower four-barrel carburettor set-up, Cher's was the mere 200 horsepower, two-barrel carb version. The Mustangs exist to this day and now live in the Midwest Dream Car Collection museum in Manhattan, Kansas.

The K12-shape Nissan Micra was almost sold as a Smart in the US. |The Smart brand was launched in the United States in 2008, but the cars were imported and sold by Penske rather than by Mercedes itself. Penske brokered a deal with Nissan to adapt the Micra and sell it as a four door Smart, going so far as to announce their plans in 2010 with the promise that sales would start the following year. The Micra plan was cancelled in 2011 when Mercedes decided to take over the distribution of Smarts in the US.

The three diamonds that make up the Mitsubishi logo are said to represent three qualities; reliability, integrity and success.

Aston Martin's AMV8 Vantage concept of 2003, the car that previewed the V8 Vantage production car, was built in India by DC Designs of Mumbai. Despite its name, the show car was based upon the guts of an old V12-powered DB7 Vantage Volante.

The last project undertaken by the Abingdon-based MG engineering team - led by Don Hayter, 'the father of the MGB' - was developing and testing 'Project Bounty', the lightly modified Honda Ballade that became the Triumph Acclaim. The team's Abingdon home was shut down during the project so they were transferred to Cowley where the car would be made and then disbanded when their work was complete.

In the 1990s the Austin/Rover Montego was sold in New Zealand as the MG Sedan and MG Estate. The cars were available with locally-developed air-con.

The longest-reigning car company boss in history is Osamu Suzuki who for 43 years ran, you guessed it, Suzuki. Having joined the company in 1958, Suzuki-san became CEO and president in 1978, then chairman and president in 2000. In 2015 he handed the job of president to his son, Toshihiro, but remained the chairman, a position he occupied until his retirement in 2021 at the age of 91.

During development of the Volvo 850 it was realised that 45 percent of the company's customers in its biggest market, the USA, were women yet the car's design team was mostly male. So 30 women from the design and product planning departments were asked for their help in giving a more 'female look' to the car which resulted in some of the harder edges of the exterior being softened off.

In the early sixties France and Germany placed extra duty on chicken imported from the United States and in January 1964 the US retaliated with swingeing tariffs on four things imported from Europe in large quantities; dextrin, brandy, potato starch and "motor vehicles for the transport of goods with a gross weight up to 8500 pounds and a payload of up to 4000 pounds". The tariffs on the dextrin, brandy and starch were subsequently repealed but to this day all light goods vehicles imported into the US are subject to a 25 percent "chicken tax". That's why every Japanese-made Subaru BRAT entering the US came with a pair of rear-facing plastic chairs bolted to the pick-up bed, enabling it to qualify as a passenger car rather than a light truck. For the same reason, when Ford started selling the Turkish-made Transit Connect in the US in 2009 each van arrived on American soil with rear side windows and a pair of flimsy back seats and was then passed through a dedicated facility in Baltimore which replaced the rear glass with metal, ripped out the seats, and blanked over the rear footwells to leave a level cargo floor. In 2013 US Customs and Border Protection issued a ruling demanding that Ford stop these shenanigans, saying "it is clear the Connect is a commercial vehicle" and forcing the company to start paying the 25 percent tariff. Ford successfully appealed this ruling and continues to import the second-generation Transit Connect, now made in Spain, with temporary back windows and extra seats.

In 2006 Citroën announced a bespoke garage for its flagship C6 saloon. The garage, designed by 'creative production company' Neutral, was conceived "to present the C6 in a truly unique and independent environment". To that end, the skeleton of the garage was made of "light transmitting concrete" and finished off with large panes of transparent polycarbonate which could turn opaque on the activation of "privacy mode". Neutral said the garage "encourages a visual dialogue between the inside and outside, and between the car and its environment as a result of the use of materials of different transparencies." The garage existed only as a series of renderings, though Citroën claimed you could order one for just £95,600 plus VAT. There's no evidence that anyone did.

The one-off Aston Martin Victor was developed under the codename 'Muncher', taken from the nickname given to the RHAM1, a privately developed Aston racer which competed at Le Mans in 1977 and '79. The original Muncher got its nickname because of an enormous appetite for brake discs.

In 1981 the South Korean government ordered Kia to stop making cars. The ruling powers, led by unelected military dictator Chun Doo-hwan, wanted to rationalise the nation's over-capacity industries and cut down on the number of car makers so they instructed Kia, at the time building the Mazda Familia, Fiat 132 and Peugeot 604 under licence, to cease car production and focus only on vans. In 1984 the government decided it would let Kia re-join the South Korean car industry and the result was a new deal with Ford which led to the Kia Pride of 1987, a badge-engineered version of the Mazda-designed Ford Festiva.

The Honda S500 was the first Japanese car ever to be available in red. Prior to its launch in 1963 red (and white) cars were illegal in Japan for fear they would be confused with emergency vehicles. During development of the S360, the aborted roadster design that led to the larger, more powerful S500, Soichiro Honda decided he wanted his new sports car to be available in vibrant red paint and lobbied the Ministry of Transportation to relax the rules, writing in a national newspaper, "Red is the basic colour of design. How can they ban it by law? I'm aware of no other industrial nation in the world in which the state monopolizes the use of colours". The government relented, Honda was able to paint its new cars red, and other Japanese car makers followed suit.

The runout version of the Renault 4 was a special edition called the Bye-Bye.

Contrary to popular belief, the BMW logo wasn't designed to depict a spinning propeller. The blue and white quarters at its centre, first used on the badge in 1917, are taken from the flag of Bavaria, though reversed to avoid breaching a contemporary law that forbad the use of state symbols on commercial logos. In 1929 BMW ran an illustration showing its logos within the spinning propellers of two BMW-powered aeroplanes and from then on it was assumed this was what the badge had been depicting all along, something the company did nothing to deny.

The grille of the first BMW Mini was inspired by that of the post-1967 original Mini but with a horizontal split through the middle so that, according to designer Frank Stephenson, the car appeared to have an 'underbite' like a bulldog.

The Ford Racing Puma was going to be called the Puma ST160. That was the name of the concept version and can be found on certain Racing-specific parts of the car including the unique front springs.

When Rover launched the third-generation 200 in 1995 it was widely reported that the car was based on the Anglo-Japanese chassis of the previous 200/400, but with an all-British torsion beam rear axle taken from the Maestro. This wasn't strictly true for two reasons. Firstly, the specific rear end used was the slightly beefier torsion beam from the Montego estate. Secondly, this design wasn't all-British as BL engineers on the LM10/11 project that became the Maestro and Montego openly copied it from Volkswagen. Their naked cribbing included buying a Polo rear axle and installing it under an Allegro to begin proving trials as well as using mk1 Jettas fitted with their own engines as engineering mules.

The S in Jaguar XJ-S stood for 'special' but also, according to Jaguar claims at the car's launch, for five other s-words; style, silence, safety, strength and speed.

The re-hashed Tata Indica of 2003 wasn't the first time the name CityRover had been used in the British car industry. At the start of the eighties there was a plan to replace the old FX4 taxi with a new design which used a Rover SD1 chassis clothed in a modified Range Rover shell and powered by a Land Rover diesel engine. It was codenamed CR6, the CR standing for City Rover. The new cab project was in development for a few years, and prototypes were papped on test at Austin Rover's Gaydon proving ground, before spiralling costs killed it in 1985.

The AMC Pacer, developed under the codename 'Project Amigo', was the length of a compact car but much wider than any rival, the idea being that width equalled prestige. AMC really hammered home this point with the original tag lines for the car which included "You only ride like a Pacer if you're wide like a Pacer", "Small was never this wide", and "The first wide small car".

The Citroën CX was notably smaller than the car it replaced, the DS, being 160mm shorter (over six inches) and 61mm narrower (almost two and a half inches) than its predecessor.

The Dukes of Hazzard has given us many things including the 'J.D.' in the name of UK pub chain J.D. Wetherspoon which is taken from Boss Hogg's initials. The character's full name was Jefferson Davis Hogg. (For the record, Wetherspoon was the surname of a man who taught the pub chain's founder Tim Martin at school.)

In 2006 an Aussie car collector paid $187,900 for the very last Holden Monaro made. Except, it wasn't technically the last Monaro made at all, only the last car to be badged as a Monaro. The actual last car of this shape was an American export model, badged as a Pontiac GTO and shipped off to the US to be sold as normal without any end-of-the-line fanfare.

When it was launched in France in 1990 the first-generation Renault Clio came in three trim levels - RL, RN and RT - with the second letters standing for Low, Normale and Top respectively.

The first Ford Focus RS was built on the same production line as lesser Focuses but to ensure it fitted with existing production processes and didn't disrupt the flow of the line each car left the factory with basic seats, no bumpers and the turbocharger installed but not connected before being shipped to an outside facility to be finished off. Its widened track wouldn't fit down the normal line either so for the first stage of production every RS rolled on a set of special reusable temporary wheels which Ford had made to fit the right stud pattern, based around Audi space saver wheels which were narrow steelies still big enough to clear the RS-spec brakes.

Until the 1970s BMW created its full-size styling models out of wood and plaster rather than faster and more flexible clay, largely because Ford and Opel hogged German supplies of suitable modelling clay preventing the BMW studio from making the switch. That is until 1971 when Bob Lutz arrived as BMW's executive vice president of sales and was horrified to discover not only the terrible in-house design for the 2002 replacement but also the slow and archaic way in which it had been created. His solution was get in touch with an old colleague at GM and from there was able to poach a few Opel design staff along with some of their supplies of clay so the car could be re-designed with fresh eyes and using more modern techniques. The result was the E21 3 Series.

The Toyota Corolla hatchback you can buy in Japan is broadly the same as the one you can buy in the Europe. However, while Japanese-market Corolla saloons and estates look at first glance like the Euro models they're actually 135mm and 155mm shorter respectively and use the same wheelbase as the hatchback where

European saloons and estates have a 60mm wheelbase stretch. The best explanation for this is that in Japan Toyota offers a greater range of saloons and estates so Corollas of these body styles can afford to be less spacious because if you need more room there'll be something else in the showroom to stop you turning to a rival car maker.

Hyundai claims the motorised charging port on its IONIQ 5 opens in 1.3 seconds, 0.2 seconds faster than the equivalent flap on the Tesla Model 3.

The updated Aston Martin V8 introduced at the Birmingham Motor Show in 1978 was known within the company as the OI, standing for 'October Introduction' after the month when the show would take place. To make the name sound sexier Aston adopted the NATO alphabet words for O and I and to this day this model is referred to as the Oscar India.

The Austin Allegro and the Chevrolet Corvette C4 have the same wheelbase.* In 2012 this fact inspired an outfit calling themselves Allegro Motorsport to meld together a 1977 Austin Allegro and a stroked-out 1989 Chevrolet Corvette to create a V8-powered, Allegro-shaped monster painted in Castrol colours. (*Well, almost. 2440mm for the 'Vette, 2438mm for the Allegro, but what's two millimetres between cars of wildly different performance and appearance?)

When the heavily revised Rover Metro was launched in 1990 most models in the range had no separate dampers, relying on the inherent damping of the newly-interconnected Hydragas suspension, but the 95bhp GTi model came with separate dampers on the front axle only, supposedly to the benefit of handling.

The Lexus 'Climate Concierge' system, introduced on the LS in 2012, uses infra-red sensors to monitor the temperature of occupants' faces and adjust the cabin temperature accordingly.

The first four-wheel-drive car to compete in the Le Mans 24 Hours was the Porsche 961 which came seventh in the 1986 race. The 959-based 961 competed in the experimental GTX category since Porsche had yet to build the 200 959s that would homologate it for Group B classification. It took part again in 1987 with less success, retiring after crashing and then catching fire, never to race again. The car was rebuilt, however, and now lives in the Porsche museum.

One of the brothers who founded Domino's Pizza traded his half of the company for a second-hand VW Beetle. In 1960 Tom and James Monaghan bought a pizza restaurant in Ypsilanti, Michigan but after eight months James decided to stick to his day job as a postman and traded his half of the business to his brother in return for a 1959 Beetle. In 1998 Tom Monaghan sold Domino's for one billion dollars. It's not known if James still has the Beetle.

For greater body rigidity the Toyota GR Yaris has 259 extra spot welds in its shell compared to a normal Yaris, making a total of 4175. The shell also contains 35.4 metres of structural adhesive, 14.6m more than in the regular Yaris.

For the last two years of its life, from November 1984 until end of production in December 1986, the Ford Capri was made exclusively in right-hand-drive and sold only in the UK and Ireland.

At the start of the eighties Aston Martin almost bought MG. BL announced it was killing the MGB and Midget and shutting down the Abingdon factory in September 1979, prompting a consortium led by Aston's owners to leap into action, claiming a war chest of £30m with which they would buy the MG name, factory and the rights to the MGB which they would keep making in updated form. To this end, Aston bought a brown MGB roadster direct from BL and let its tame designer, William Towns, give the car a facelift consisting of new bumpers, new wheels, a lightly revised interior and, most significantly, the taller windscreen from the MGB GT. In just a week, Aston staff at Newport Pagnell re-built the car to Towns's spec and re-sprayed it gold before it was shown off to the press in June 1980. Unfortunately, negotiations faltered shortly afterwards and the deal was off. The last MGB left the doomed Abingdon production line in October 1980. The Aston-modified MGB was sold off in 1984 and lives on in private hands to this day.

During development of the Volvo 480 engineers realised that they couldn't accommodate adequate guides to keep the door glass in place without adding a little triangle to the trailing edge of each front window. Unhappy about this, chief designer Rob Koch decided to make the best of it by insisting the little triangle was painted matt black and that the engineers moved the door lock onto it so that owners didn't scratch the paint on the door when unlocking their cars. That's how the 480 ended up with its unusual lock-above-the-handle door layout.

The Kitten was the first Reliant with rectangular headlights.

The British buy more convertible cars than any other European country which might explain why the Renault Wind went on sale in the UK four months before it was available in its native France.

In 1974 Mercedes started developing project W201, the car that became the 190, but wanted to hide its plans for an all-new 'baby Benz' compact saloon for as long as possible. That's why early testing was carried out using 190 underparts grafted beneath cut 'n' shut shells from old W114 saloons and when visually representative prototypes came along they wore a different nose with bland horizontal slats instead of a full M-B chrome grille, generic tail lights, Ford Granada wheel trims, fake badges that read 'Ushido' and even Opel steering wheels to throw off anyone glancing at the interior. To complete the deception, these cars were registered in the Bavarian city of Augsburg, miles from Merc's base in Stuttgart and rather closer to BMW's home in Munich. The ruse didn't work that well because in 1977, five years before the 190 was made official, Auto Zeitung magazine papped one of these test cars and correctly identified it as the new compact Benz.

The AMC Pacer was intended to have a Wankel rotary engine. In February 1973 AMC signed a deal with American aeronautical and defence corporation Curtiss-Wright (who co-owned the rights to the Wankel alongside NSU) so that they could develop a rotary engine of their own. Then, realising this might be quite time consuming, they came up with a stop-gap plan to buy Wankels from GM which had been working on such engines for years. When GM abruptly cancelled its Wankel programme in 1974 this left AMC with little prospect of getting a rotary suitable for production any time soon and the company was forced to cram its existing straight six into the Pacer ready for the car's launch in February 1975.

The Chrysler Sunbeam was developed at breakneck speed, driven by a need to keep the company's Linwood plant in Scotland alive by giving it something new to make. The project was conceived in December 1975 and given the go ahead in January 1976. The car's styling was approved in February 1976, all the engineering signed off two weeks later, and by October '76 prototypes were running before the first pilot-build cars came off the line in January '77, just one year after the car was given the go ahead by management. In April 1977 the first cars from production tooling were made and the car was launched that July. Even by modern standards, and even for a car based on a cutdown platform of an existing model (in this case the chassis of the Avenger saloon), a 19-month gestation is pretty bloody brisk. The model lasted for just under four years, during which time around 200,000 were made. The last Sunbeam, by then badged a Talbot, was built in May 1981 after which the Linwood factory closed down.

The original codename of the Citroën 2 CV was TPV standing for Très Petite Voiture or Very Small Car.

The one-off Aston Martin Bulldog was hastily switched to be left- rather than right-hand-drive during its construction because the Sultan of Oman agreed to buy the car it once it had been finished and shown off to the world in March 1980. He then dropped out of the deal and the car stayed at Aston Martin until 1984 when it was sold to Prince Muhammed bin Saud of Saudi Arabia.

CARS WITH PORTMANTEAU NAMES

Alfa Romeo MiTo – Milano, Torino
Daewoo Leganza – elegante e forza
Hyundai Ioniq – Ion, unique
Hyundai Veloster – Velocity, roadster*
Mitsubishi Starion – star of Orion**
Nissan Pulsar – pulsating star
Porsche Boxster – boxer roadster
Renault Avantime – avant time
Renault Twingo – twist, swing et tango
Renault Vel Satis – vélocité et satisfaction
Volkswagen Tiguan – Tiger, Leguan***

* No, it's not actually a roadster.
** Urban legend has it that Starion comes from a mispronunciation of 'stallion' but there's no concrete evidence of this and Mitsubishi maintains the official explanation above.
*** The German for iguana.

Speaking of portmanteaux, in the early 1970s Mazda's UK importer wanted to stress that the company's products combined quality with luxury and performance and, as such, were 'QLP cars'. But that wasn't catchy enough so they ran ads in which the headline was simply, 'QUALUXANCE'. Strangely, this word never caught on. Maybe because it's not a word, it's just bollocks.

General Motors was delighted with the success of Knight Rider, starring its latest Pontiac Firebird Trans Am, and quickly made plans for a special Knight Rider edition model that looked like K.I.T.T. According to series creator Glen A. Larson, this scheme was promptly nixed after the GM board heard of a man in New Orleans who was planning to jump over a train in his Trans Am and had a panic about liabilities if the company sold a car with explicit links to the leaping Pontiac in the TV show.

To develop the original Freelander's complicated side-hinged tailgate with its frameless, retractable glass, Land Rover engineers fitted the mechanism to a specially modified Discovery which was badged as a Honda Crossroad, the re-labelled Discovery sold only in Japan, to confuse casual onlookers intrigued by its weird-looking back door.

Volvo offshoot Polestar might seem Swedish but its efforts to date, the Polestar 1 and Polestar 2, have been built in China and some of the company's engineering happens at a satellite R&D centre in Coventry, UK.

The driving in Renault's Papa and Nicole adverts was done by rally driver and Driven presenter Penny Mallory. It was rumoured at the time that Estelle Skornik who played Nicole couldn't actually drive, though in 1998 she strongly refuted this in an interview with The Independent, insisting that she passed her test when she was 18, two years before the first Clio ad was filmed.

Legendary Mancunian music producer Martin Hannett wasn't famed for his level-headed lifestyle choices, not least his enthusiastic consumption of heroin, but when it came to transport his tastes were surprisingly sensible. "He loved Volvo cars," recalls Magazine's keyboard player and Hannett's friend, Dave Formula. In his excellent book Fast Forward, Joy Division and New Order drummer Stephen Morris confirms Hannett's enthusiasm for Swedish steel, quoting him as saying, "Good crashing car, the Volvo. Acres of metal and heated seats."

Among its many unique parts, the Metro 6R4 had windscreen washer jets built into its wiper arms where standard Metro screen washers squirted from a (less effective) plastic blob on the scuttle panel.

In Russia the Lada Niva is available from the factory with camouflage paint. It's a £285 option. Quite pricey when metallic paint is only £90. But it's proper paint rather than a wrap, so that's nice.

Despite having different glasshouse profiles, the three- and five-door versions of the first Range Rover Evoque shared the same roof pressing. The five-door had a taller windscreen and the roof tapered less towards the rear where it met a deeper tailgate but the actual roof panel was the same, delivering a handy cost saving.

The building in the infamous 'Britischer Architekt' TV ad for the Rover 800 Fastback of 1988 is the Neue Staatsgalerie, an art gallery in Stuttgart designed by James Stirling who was, obviously, a British architect.

According to Skoda it took 1187 new parts to turn the Favorit into the heavily revised Felicia of 1994. The company described this comprehensive facelift as a "technically demanding re-development".

The first special edition of the Vauxhall Calibra was the Tickford of 1991. Based on either the 2.0 8v or 2.0 16v, each Vauxhall Tickford Calibra came with unique alloys, Tickford badges, part Alcantara seats, a new design of leather steering wheel, a leather gearlever gaiter, footwell lights, Tickford tread plates, and a leather-lined cubby on the passenger side. Just 26 were made. The most successful Calibra special edition was the SE of 1992-93 which was based on the 2.0 8v and came with Caribic Blue metallic paint, unique 15-inch alloys, velour seats (or optional leather), a leather steering wheel and branded velour floor mats. "Enjoy the style, comfort and performance" said the brochure, and over 1800 people decided to give that a try. It was such a hit that another eight limited run Calibra SE variations followed.

In 1988, as part of the Range Rover's inexorable rise upmarket, Land Rover introduced a new, extra luxurious model called the Vogue SE which featured air-conditioning, electric sunroof, electrically adjustable leather seats, extra sound proofing, and bodywork in either Caspian Blue or Cypress Green with alloys painted the same colour. The new model's atmosphere of sophistication and attention to detail was somewhat undermined by one of the beautifully lit brochure shots in which the front tyres were of two different types and clearly didn't match.

The name Hyundai comes from 'hyeondae', the Korean word for 'the present age'.

In 2014 Nissan sold a limited-run version of the GT-R called the Gentleman Edition. Available only in gunmetal grey with an amber red interior, the Gentleman Edition featured additional hand-stitched leather interior trimmings, a numbered titanium dashboard plaque, a leather Gentleman Edition overnight bag and matching glasses case. How gentlemanly. The Gentleman Edition was only available in France and Belgium and just 10 were made, one for each GT-R centre across the two countries.

The very last Volkswagen Corrado ever made was right-hand-drive. The car, a VR6 Storm in Classic Green, now lives in the VW museum.

Almost 330,000 Rover P6s were built during the model's 13½ year production span yet only 47 of them had metallic paint. This is because the P6 was sold exclusively with non-metallic paint until 1976 when Rover announced it was building 77 'VIP' special editions, one for each of its British dealers. The high-spec VIP came with fancy features like air-conditioning and velour upholstery, previewing the fabric that would be used to trim the insides of the forthcoming SD1. On the outside the VIP was available in non-metallic Brasilia brown or a brand-new paint planned to be used on the SD1, metallic Platinum silver. Of the run of 77 cars, 30 were brown leaving the rest as the only metallic P6s ever sold.

At the time of writing Ferrari sells as many different series production models in the UK as Fiat. It's six each. For Ferrari there's the Portofino M, Roma, F8 Tributo/Spider, 296 GTB, SF90 Stradale/Spider and 812 Superfast/GTS. For Fiat, the Panda, 500, 500e, 500X, 500L and Tipo. If you include limited production specials such as the 812 Competizione, Monza SP1 and Monza SP2 then Ferrari actually has a wider model range than Fiat.

Princess Diana was a serial Ford Escort mk3 driver, starting with a silver 1.6 Ghia given to her by Prince Charles in May 1981. In June 2021 this car sold for £47,000 at auction. The five door Ghia was replaced by a red 1.6i Cabriolet, prompting concerns from the Metropolitan Police's Royalty Protection Group, SO14, which felt the colour and the drop top made it too conspicuous. Diana agreed to switch to another Escort hatchback but wanted the racy RS Turbo version which, to the Met's chagin, only came in attention grabbing bright white. To solve this problem, Ford PR man Harry Calton organised a special-order Turbo made in low profile black with the five slat grille from lesser Escorts instead of the Turbo's unique three slatter, a low-key effect slightly undermined by the bright blue side stripes and RS decals. However, Diana's RS Turbo wasn't the only example of this model made in black because SO14 asked Ford for two further identical cars, one to use as a decoy and one for another, unnamed member of the Royal family.

Norway's enthusiastic adoption of electric cars can be attributed to local pop group A-ha. In 1989 singer Morten Harket and keyboardist Mags Furuholmen, along with Norwegian environmentalist Frederic Hauge, visited an EV show in Switzerland and came across a Fiat Panda converted to electric power. They bought the car and took it back to Norway where they found that under the rules of the time it was impossible to register it as an electric vehicle. Since it had a propane heater like a motorhome they registered it instead as a diesel RV and then, to make a point about how the rules needed to change, set about driving it around without paying any of the road tolls for which it was liable. This incurred a 300 Krone fine which Harket, Furuholmen and Hauge refused to pay so the car was confiscated in lieu of payment and sent to auction... where the cheeky popsters simply bought it back again for 200 Krone and carried on driving it, still without paying tolls. This cycle continued, drawing enormous publicity, until the Norwegian authorities gave in and in 1996 EVs became exempt from road tax and toll charges, laying the foundations for the incentivised popularity of electric cars in Norway today.

During development of the third-generation Dacia Sandero the car's designers wanted to put the radio aerial in a fashionable position at the rear of the roof. Dacia's iron-fisted cost controllers didn't like the sound of this since it would require a longer and more expensive wire in each example. In the end the designers re-designed the dashboard layout, saving on wiring costs there, and then 'spent' that saving on the aerial position they wanted.

The 1980 Chevrolet Citation may have been a little-loved large hatchback with a terrible reputation for lousy dynamics and wonky build quality but on the plus side it was also partly responsible for the brilliant five-cylinder engine that powered the 1991 Volvo 850. When Volvo engineers started work on the new engine and gearbox in the early eighties they needed a car in which to install the engine for proving trials and management demonstrations. Actual 850 prototypes were a long way off and nothing in their current range could easily take a transverse five-cylinder engine and gearbox driving the front wheels without a lot of modification. Engineers alighted on the FWD Citation, bought one, installed their own powertrain, and the success of this mule made from an otherwise miserable car was enough to get the five-cylinder motor signed off for further development.

The Mercedes R-Class died without replacement in 2013, except in China where it was actually quite popular and remained on sale until 2017. At first Merc met this unexpected Chinese demand by keeping the R-Class line going at its Alabama factory but from 2015 onwards the car was exclusively assembled under contract in Indiana by AM General, the people behind the Hummer.

In October 1996 Peugeot launched a home-market special edition of the 106 called the Cartoon which featured car-shaped headrests, roughly mimicking the profile of the car itself. The generous equipment list also including electric windows, remote central locking, and a luridly multi-coloured seat fabric design called 'Bugs et Bugsy'. The Cartoon limited edition was such a hit that it came back again in February 1998 and then again in January 1999. The model was even given an animated TV ad campaign featuring Tex Avery characters Droopy, Wolf and Red Hot Riding Hood. In 2021 Peugeot put out a press release to mark 30 years of the 106 in which the Cartoon special edition was described as "very fun".

From 1 January 2021 Chevrolet had to stop selling the high performance ZL1, SS and 1LE versions of the Camaro because of their brakes, but only in California and Washington. These models featured copper in their brake pads, breaching laws passed in 2010 in both states which, for environmental reasons, decreed no more than five percent copper in vehicle brakes by 2021. So Chevrolet stopped taking orders for these models in these two states until it could phase in new brake pads with a legal level of copper content.

While Vauxhall wanted to sell an estate version of the mk2 Cavalier, colleagues at Opel in Germany had no interest in such a bodystyle for their sister car, the Ascona. Fortunately Holden had come up with a wagon version of the Camira, their saloon built on the same GM J-body platform, so Vauxhall did a deal to buy rear body stampings for the estate shell and import them all the way from Australia to their Luton assembly plant to make the Cavalier estate possible.

In the mid-eighties Renault assigned 180,000,000 Francs (about £45m in today's money) to Federalising the Alpine GTA so that it could be sold in the US. Changes included a more luxurious interior with standard air-conditioning, around 200 kilos of additional crash protection measures including larger bumpers, and pop-up headlights rather than fixed lamps under glass covers (the latter being illegal under US law at the time). The project was completed in 1987, just in time for Renault to beat a retreat from the American market rendering the whole endeavour pointless. Though not entirely a waste of time because, of the 21 US-spec GTAs completed, 12 were sold to private customers in France and the rest were used to develop an updated Euro GTA which included many of the Federal measures such as pop-up lights and side impact beams. This new model reached European showrooms in 1991 as the Alpine A610.

Land Rover South Africa sold a locally developed and built version of the Defender powered by a BMW straight six. The car came about thanks to a BMW engineer called Frank Isenberg who was working in South Africa during BMW's ownership of Rover Group and, after encountering a Defender 110 at a BMW SA facility, began to suspect the then-new 2.8-litre M52 six might make a more economical alternative to the Land Rover's old 3.5-litre V8. After a bit of tape measuring he became convinced the engine would fit, got colleagues in Munich and Solihull on board to supply parts to make an experimental transplant possible, and within three weeks had a prototype running to such convincing effect that it was eventually signed off for production. The Defender 2.8i was made at BMW's factory in Rosslyn between 1997 and 2001, during which time just under 1400 were sold. Frank Isenberg, meanwhile, went on to become chief engineer on the BMW 1M and M2, and, many years later while browsing online ads from his home in Munich, found a red Defender 2.8i for sale in South Africa which he bought for himself.

The Datsun Fairlady sports car of 1960 was so-called because company president Katsuji Kawamata heard about the successful Broadway musical My Fair Lady and decided such a name would sound exotic and cool in Japan. Really running with the theme, Datsun also recruited attractive women to act as sales people at the company's showroom in Tokyo's fashionable Ginza distract and called them 'Miss Fairladys'. The range of Fairlady sports cars carried on throughout the sixties and in 1969 a brand new six-cylinder coupé arrived, called the Fairlady Z. The Z was added because it was the last letter of the alphabet and therefore defined this model as 'the last word in sports cars'. Fortunately, when Datsun decided to sell this car in the United States the mastermind behind it, Yutaka Katayama, realised that while its name worked well in Japan it sounded like absolute toss to English-speaking ears and lobbied to have the car re-named using its 2.4-litre engine capacity as inspiration while keeping the flourish of the Z. And that's how the 240Z came about.

Holden officially ceased to exist as a company on 31 December 2020.

Although the last generation of the Ford Cortina is commonly referred to as the Mk5, at launch its official name within Ford was 'Cortina 80', so-called because it was a heavy facelift of the Mk4 and released in autumn '79, just in time for the arrival of 1980.

Concept cars have had cameras instead of side mirrors for years but the first production car to reach showrooms with this technology was the Japanese-market Lexus ES of 2018, just beating the Audi e-tron.

Porsche nerds sometimes refer to the Turbo version of the 964-shape 911 as the 965 but this isn't correct. The actual 965 project was an ambitious attempt to make a 'baby 959' which would have sat above the 964 Carrera being developed in parallel during the mid-eighties. After the economic crash of 1987 Porsche sales collapsed and the company realised it couldn't afford such extravagance, the 965 was cancelled, and in its place came a hasty plan to install the old 930 engine into the 964 shell to create a new flagship. The lesser-known codename for this project was Typ 994.

The Renault Magnum truck was styled by the man who designed the Lamborghini Countach. Marcello Gandini's other credits include the Lancia Stratos, the Citroën BX and the Cizeta-Moroder V16T.

At its launch in 1984 the Austin Montego had clever column stalks with symbols that illuminated at night by means of fibre optics running inside, carrying light from a bulb within the steering column. This ingenious idea was deleted in 1988.

SAAB's first production car, the 92 of 1949, was originally available only in one shade of green because the company had lots of this paint left over from building military aircraft during the Second World War. Later in the car's life they began to introduce new colours, some confected by Swedish abstract painter Pierre Olofsson who was friends with SAAB chief designer Sixten Sason. One of Olofsson's contributions was a new shade of green, the genesis of which he explained as follows; "You take one part cream, one part cheap brandy and one part green Chartreuse. Tastes bloody awful, but man what a marvellous colour".

The Toyota GR Yaris has special covers that cap off the ends of its undertrays to prevent dirt and stones from getting into them. This unusual feature was introduced after testing on gravel.

Between 1969 and 1971 BMC Australia sold a unique, locally-built version of the Mini which, unlike UK-made Minis of the time, had a 1098cc version of the A-series engine and was badged as the Mini K. The K stood for Kangaroo, as indicated by the special kangaroo stickers ahead of the doors and a punsome advertising slogan which called it a "great leap forward". The abbreviated Kangaroo name might have been chosen to reinforce that the car was claimed to be made of 80 percent local content, although some believe it was also to boast of the car's minimal thirst since actual kangaroos can survive for long periods without drinking.

The TVR Griffith gets its name from American Ford dealer Jack Griffith, the man who decided to pull the weedy MG four-cylinder from a TVR Grantura and replace it with a small-block Ford V8. From this the original Griffith 200 of 1965 was born, and TVR honoured the name with the new Griffith of 1991.

Mazda no longer sells the amusingly named Bongo Friendee minivan in Japan but since 2019 it has offered a domestic market commercial vehicle called the Bongo Brawny. It's just a re-badged Toyota HiAce.

Mercedes could have had a small hatchback a good 15 years before the A-Class. In the early eighties the company built a prototype based around the cutdown platform of the then-secret 190 compact saloon, primarily as an experiment into creating a short-wheelbase rally machine but also to test the water for the feasibility an even smaller Merc. The experimental car was disguised like early 190 prototypes with a plain rectangular grille, Granada wheel trims and a Cologne registration to fool people into thinking it was an unreleased Ford but the crudely adapted S123 tailgate and rear lights gave the game away and the press weren't fooled when the car was papped on test in 1981. The project was binned when Benz bosses decided the world wasn't ready for a Merc hatchback and that a rear-drive, 190-based rally car would be pointless against the new four-wheel-drive Audi Quattro. A prototype, now wearing 190 alloys and a Stuttgart plate, survives in Mercedes' museum, billed as the 190E Stadtwagen (city car).

There have been rap tracks that reference Range Rovers, Bentleys and Maybachs but only 'Citroën' by Parisian singer and rapper Lomepal namechecks the Citroën AX and obscure Romanian-made eighties three-door the Citroën Axel before ending on the lines, "Yeah, it rolls like my old Citroën BX / And I'll stick it out for everything / A Citroën BX still rolls". He probably means 'rolls' in the sense of 'drives' rather than making some statement about the axial rotation of the body caused by weight transfer during cornering.

Not to be outdone in the unusual car namecheck stakes, in 2019 Californian hip-hop artist Hobo Johnson released a track called 'Subaru Crosstrek XV' the chorus of which goes, "I just bought a Subaru

Crosstrek / I woulda bought a Lambo, but I'm not quite there yet".

For many years the British Motor Industry Heritage Trust displayed an Avocado green Rover 3500S which was described as the last Rover P6 ever made. In fact, this car was built some months prior to the end of production and was hastily 'finished off' on the line as it closed in March 1977 before being anointed as the last of the breed. As if to acknowledge that this 3500S wasn't as special as claimed, in 2003 the Heritage museum sold it.

Honda has used the name Jazz three times. On the Euro versions of the City and then, more recently, the Fit. But also, between 1993 and 1996, as the name for their re-badged Isuzu MU (known in the UK as the Vauxhall Frontera) sold only through Honda dealers in Japan.

If you haven't got a tape measure handy to check the wheelbase, a quick way to establish if a 1990s Z32 Nissan 300ZX is the two-seater or the 2+2 version is to look at the location of the fuel filler. On the shorter car it's ahead of the rear wheel, on the four-seater it's behind it. Also, two seaters could have a solid or lift-out roof, 2+2s came only with the targa top. Alternatively, you could peek through the rear window to see if the car you're looking at has back seats. That would be another way of checking, obviously.

The Aston Martin Bulldog concept car was named after the Scottish Aviation Bulldog, a light aircraft flown by Alan Curtis, managing director and part-owner of Aston at the time. A keen aviator, Curtis also owned Compton Abbas airfield in Dorset.

The original Twingo of 1992 would be signed off for production only if Renault engineers could make major cost savings in the way it was built. One of the results of their drive for simplification was that, at launch, the car came with only one engine, one trim level and a choice of just four paint colours. Designing it around a single, relatively low-powered engine created a virtuous circle in which suspension and braking systems could be simpler and therefore cheaper, safe in the knowledge they wouldn't have to handle greater power outputs, and there were myriad cost-saving details like a simplified seat design using fabric bonded straight to the foam and a radio aerial mounted on the door mirror not the roof, reducing the amount of wiring needed. Many of the cost reduction tricks learnt from the Twingo project came in handy when designing the first Dacia Logan.

At the end of the sixties Triumph began developing a high-performance version of the upcoming Dolomite under the codename 'Project Swift'. For production, however, it was intended to call it the Dolomite 135 to reflect the power output of its innovative 16-valve engine. Unfortunately, a delay in getting the car on sale coincided with a shift from SAE to DIN standards for measuring official horsepower numbers and under the new procedure the production engine's official output came in at 127bhp. As a result Triumph honourably abandoned the 135 name, despite already having badges made, and the car arrived in showrooms newly re-named as the Dolomite Sprint.

The American-market Merkur XR4Ti might have looked much like the European Sierra XR4i that spawned it but under the skin it had over 100 kilos of additional metalwork to meet Federal safety standards and a Brazilian-made 2.3-litre turbo four-cylinder instead of the Cologne V6 of the Euro car. In fact, it was so different that it couldn't be made economically on the Sierra production line and XR4Tis were instead assembled by Karmann in Osnabrück.

Despite being the most successful car of the late Group B rally era, the Peugeot 205 T16 had one insurmountable flaw; it 'flew' lopsided over yumps and landed unpredictably, an unfixable characteristic which came from its transverse engine being mounted asymmetrically.

Robert 'Maximum Bob' Lutz has overseen the creation of many interesting cars including the original BMW 3 Series, the first Dodge Viper, and the re-born Chevy Camaro but the project he claims to be most proud of is the Ford Sierra.

One of the great clichés of car design is that a given model has been styled to 'look like it's moving even when it's standing still'. This old trope was subverted by Land Rover chief designer Andy Wheel who used to joke that the Discovery 3, a car meant to look architectural and planted, was designed to 'look like it's standing still even when it's moving'.

Trevor Fiore, designer of the Alpine A310 and DeTomaso Vallelunga, was born Trevor Frost in Sheffield. After starting his design career at Standard Triumph in Coventry he got a job with Fissore in Milan and changed his surname to the more carrozzeria-compatible Fiore which was the family name of his Italian mother.

The Fiat Panda 100HP had 99bhp.

Between 1999 and 2015 the font on Apple keyboards was VAG Rundschrift, a bespoke typeface originally created for Volkswagen. VW commissioned VAG Rundschrift ('VAG Rounded' in English) as a way of unifying corporate identity across the whole group and used it from 1979 onwards before phasing it out from 1990 onwards after deciding that each company within the group should have its own, separate look. Once VW had released VAG Rundschrift into the public domain other companies to use it included MySpace and Skype.

When Top Gear was re-booted in 2002 the title sequence started with a helicopter shot of six red cars driving in close formation around the test track, rising up to reveal a massive version of the show's 'cog' logo on the roof of the studio hangar. Except that from such a height the actual studio hangar looked a bit small so the logo, applied in post-production rather than painted on in real life, was applied to the much larger hangar next door. The original studio is the small building attached to the far side of the big hangar that has the logo on its roof.

The Chrysler/Talbot Sunbeam Lotus had a convoluted production process which started at the Linwood factory in Scotland where standard Sunbeam 1.6 GLS shells were given stronger suspension mounts and a larger transmission tunnel then fitted with stiffer springs and dampers and a beefier anti-roll bar on the front end before being transported to Lotus in Norfolk so the engine and gearbox could be installed. The cars were then shipped to a Chrysler/Talbot facility in Coventry for final inspection before being sent out to dealers. As a result, the Sunbeam Lotus production line was technically about 520 miles long.

The Rover Streetwise came about after MG Rover design director Peter Stevens convened one of his studio's regular Friday afternoon casual chats and asked his young designers why none of them drove the company's products. The predictable answer was because they weren't cool so Stevens challenged them to make one of the company's existing cars cooler and by the end of the afternoon they'd established a plan to make a 'dystopian urban survivors' car'. Stevens promptly nabbed a Rover 25 from somewhere within the company and the team set about re-modelling it with raised ride height, chunky cladding, tough-looking alloys and four individual seats. The designers even Photoshopped images of the car in suitably post-apocalyptic scenarios and came up with a mythical 'Streetwise' range of grungy, urban clothes to match the tone they were seeking. MG Rover's sales director loved the finished car and immediately signed it off for production but, as Stevens himself notes retrospectively, this spin-off created for a younger audience actually ended up hitting the spot with elderly rural types who liked the raised ride height because it made the car easier to get into and enjoyed the plastic cladding because it resisted scratches as they eased down narrow country lanes.

The E at the end of old school Mercedes-Benz model names stands for Einspritzung or 'injection'. The same German word is why sportiest versions of the Opel-developed Vauxhall Astra were badged GTE not GTI.

In 1979 Renault set up a small skunkworks operation called BEREX (Bureau d'Études et de Recherches Exploratoires or Exploratory Studies and Research Office). Based in Dieppe, BEREX took some of the talented people from the recently disbanded Renault Sport racing team and the brilliant minds of the Alpine research office, both also based in Dieppe, to form a crack unit that would go on to create some of France's finest sporty cars of the eighties and nineties. The first BEREX job was to take on the mad, mid-engined Renault 5 Turbo project started by the defunct Renault Sport operation and see it through to production. From there BEREX went on to create the Alpine GTA and A610, the engines for the Renault 25 V6 Turbo and the slightly crackers Safrane Biturbo, the legendary Clio Williams, and a stillborn project for a new mid-engined Alpine sportscar codenamed W71 which was cancelled after running prototypes had been made but which donated its chassis and running gear to the Renault Sport Spider. BEREX ceased to exist in 1995 when its operations were merged into other parts of Renault.

When pilot assembly of the second-generation Nissan Qashqai started at the company's UK plant in Tyne & Wear the model was still secret and each completed car had to be dressed in a checker-pattern camo wrap before being allowed out of the building for on-road testing. This almost caused a diplomatic incident at the factory because the wrap was black and white, the colours of local football team Newcastle United, causing great offence to all the plant's employees who supported other local side and hated Newcastle rivals, Sunderland. Quick thinking Nissan management neutralised this potential industrial unrest by insisting that half the pilot-build cars were henceforth wrapped in red and white camo, thereby matching the colours of the Sunderland strip.

One of the internal briefs during development of the M100 Lotus Elan of 1989 was that 90 per cent of people should be able to drive it at 90 per cent of its capability for 90 per cent of the time.

The Alpine GTA of 1984 got its name from an abbreviation of Grand Tourisme Alpine. In Britain it was called the Renault GTA because at the time Peugeot owned the UK rights to the Alpine name, an ultimately useless bonus of buying Chrysler Europe who had in turn inherited the name from Rootes which had used it since the 1950s.

The 2014 Jeep Renegade was the first Jeep-badged vehicle to be made exclusively outside of North America. US-market Renegades are assembled in Melfi, Italy while the car is also built in China and Brazil.

In December 1971 and again in January 1974 the Motor Racing Show took place on Free Enterprise II, a Townsend Thoresen car ferry which was sailed up the Thames into London and moored at Tower Pier next to Tower Bridge with various racing cars arranged on its car decks for the occasion.

The Peugeot 405 estate was 10mm shorter than the saloon.

Tuned mass dampers caused controversy during the 2006 Formula 1 season but the basic idea has long been seen in road cars. The Citroën 2 CV, for example, featured a weight on a spring inside a cylinder behind each wheel with the same intention as the mass dampers in F1 cars, to reduce the movement of the wheels in order to keep the tyres in contact with road. This system was deleted from the 2 CV in 1975. Another road car to feature a tuned mass damper was the Triumph TR7 convertible which featured weights in the front bumper designed to cancel out some of the additional bodyshell vibrations caused by the removal of the metal roof.

General Motors' Epsilon platform was a huge undertaking, designed to create one global platform for all mid-size cars made by GM subsidiaries around the world. In order to make it work, every part of it had to be as standardised as possible so that any car made anywhere in the world had the maximum possible cost-effective commonality under the skin. Even the more sophisticated and expensive suspension systems assigned to SAABs and Cadillacs were designed to bolt on to the same mounting points as the low line chassis parts used in other models. But there was one area in which GM reluctantly allowed variation and that was in, of all things, the interior lock and unlock button. North American consumers expected to find this control on the door panel while representatives from GM's European divisions insisted that drivers in their home territories were used to finding it on the centre console and both sides were so trenchant on the issue that in the end the people in charge of the Epsilon project permitted both variations to go ahead, even though this cost more because of the necessary differences in wiring looms.

After buying Rover in 1967, Leyland began experimenting with lorries powered by gas turbine engines and in 1968 boldly announced a bespoke gas turbine model with a modified Ergomatic cab re-styled by David Bache and his team from the Rover cars design studio which the company said would be in showrooms during 1970. This didn't quite go to plan, but by 1971 it had built a handful of tractor units and loaned one each to Esso, Castrol and Shell-Mex BP. It made sense to lend these trucks to oil companies since access to free fuel would be the best way to deal with these machines' sizeable appetites. In fact, it was this thirst, along with reliability issues, that saw Leyland's gas turbine project wound down by the mid-seventies. While the test trucks were scrapped an earlier prototype to the Rover studio style was saved and has now been restored.

Porsche seems to have driven into a 99x cul-de-sac for the codenames of successive 911s, starting with the 993 of 1994. That was followed by the 996 and then the 997 which was replaced, surprisingly, by the 991 before that in turn gave way to the current car, the 992. So where next, codename-wise? Well, 994 has already been used as the internal code for the 964 Turbo while 995 was a 928-based tech research project from 1978 which featured ABS and a five-speed PDK transmission wrapped in a skeletal frame rather than proper panels. That means the only 99x numbers left are 990, 998 and 999.

The Toyota GR Yaris has a roof that is 95mm lower than that of a standard Yaris. It's also made of carbon fibre rather than steel, saving 3.5kg and thereby lowering the centre-of-gravity by 2.5mm.

JAPANESE COMPANIES WHOSE BADGES
HAVE APPEARED ON CARS
MADE IN THE UK

Honda
Isuzu
Mazda
Nissan
Suzuki
Toyota

JAPANESE COMPANIES WHOSE BADGES HAVE NOT APPEARED ON CARS MADE IN THE UK

Mitsubishi
Subaru

The Chevrolet Vega, GM's 1970 attempt to beat imported compact cars at their own game, might be the only car in history to be shipped vertically. In a fit of lateral thinking, General Motors decided to find a way to cram more cars onto the trains that shipped its freshly made products across the US and the solution was a system it called 'Vert-A-Pac' in which the sides of specially modified railcars hinged down to reveal single car ramps onto which Vegas could be driven, nose-on to the train on both sides, and then tied down before the carriage sides were lifted up and closed leaving brand new cars standing on their noses, roof to roof, for their journey across the country. It wasn't just the train carriages that needed special modifications to make this bizarre system work; each Vega had to be built with four removable steel sockets on its underside to allow it to be bolted to its ramp, temporary plastic spacers to cushion the engine mounts, and myriad special features to prevent each car piddling fluids during transit including a modified carburettor to stop fuel leaking out, a baffle in the sump to avoid oil pooling in the front most cylinder and a re-located battery filler to ensure no acid escaped. Even the windscreen washer bottle was mounted at 45 degrees to avoid leaks during transit. The Vega itself turned out to be a disaster, plagued by quality and reliability problems, but Vert-A-Pac wasn't such a bad idea, allowing GM to cram 30 cars into a train carriage that could normally take no more than 18 and this saved the company a claimed 40 percent on its shipping costs. Nonetheless, the Vega was the first and only car ever to be shipped standing up.

The Lotus 340R wasn't the most practical car in the world. Not only did it have no roof and no doors but if the battery died you had to go through the time-consuming process of removing the entire body in order to replace it.

The 1981 Dubai Grand Prix wasn't an actual F1 race, more a series of demonstration events around a temporary track in the desert, billed as "the biggest motor racing event ever to hit the Arabian Gulf" and organised by Martin Hone, a former carpet salesman who would go on to arrange the Birmingham Superprix. The event included sportscar racing, saloon car racing, and demonstration laps by Juan Manuel Fangio in a Mercedes W196, Stirling Moss in a Maserati 250F and Roy Salvadori in an Aston Martin DBR4. Most bizarrely, there was a one-off, one-make race featuring some of the world's top driving talent including Richard Attwood, Derek Bell, Jack Brabham, Dan Gurney, Phil Hill, Denny Hulme, Innes Ireland, Patrick Tambay and John Watson, plus Moss and Salvatori, all driving identical cars. And the model chosen for this amazing coming together of motorsport legends? The Citroën CX. Admittedly the GTi version but even so, not the most natural racing car in the world.

The 1994 Ford GT90 concept was based on a lengthened Jaguar XJ220 chassis. Unlike the production XJ220, however, the GT90 had a V12 which was based around one-and-half V8s, garnished with four turbos for good measure. Since the GT90 was intended to be a runner this engine needed some shake-down mileage but rather than do this in a $3m one-off, Ford engineers jammed the 4.9-litre V12 into an ordinary Lincoln Town Car.

In the early nineties Indian car maker Sipani, previously responsible for a locally assembled Reliant Kitten called the Dolphin, struck a deal with Rover to sell the Montego. Under the arrangement, diesel-powered Montego saloons and estates were assembled in the UK, save for a few items like the battery and the horn, and then shipped to India to be finished off. The cars came with a lavish spec that included electric windows, power steering and a sunroof and were advertised with the slogans, "A car that spells pure luxury" and "For men who appreciate pure pleasure". Despite this, the car did not fly from showrooms, largely on account of high import duties which made it very expensive. In fact, just 500 Montegos were shipped to Sipani during 1994 and '95 and in 2005 a contributor to the Team-BHP website in India discovered a Mumbai car dealer with around a dozen of them still sitting unregistered in a compound.

The interior design of the Peugeot 205 was overseen by Paul Bracq, the man responsible for the designs of the original BMW 3 Series, 5 Series and 7 Series. Prior to BMW and Peugeot, Bracq also worked at Mercedes where he's credited as one of the people who styled the 'Grosse' 600. He arrived a BMW in 1967 and set to work on a new generation of saloons as well as the BMW Turbo concept of 1972, the styling of which evolved into the M1. Bracq left BMW in 1974, before all of his new saloons were launched, and joined Peugeot where he led the interior design of not only the 205 but also the 305, 505, 405, 106 and 406. He retired in 1996.

For the first two years of its life the original Ford Ka featured a large, round hazard warning button sunk into the far side of the stereo bezel. For 1999, however, the hazard warning trigger moved to the top of the steering column, as in most other Fords of this era, enabling the column stalk/hazard switch assembly to be shared with the Ka's platform mates, the Fiesta and Puma. This left a redundant hole in the bespoke stereo facia which was plugged by a shaped blank with the stylised Ka logo on it unless a heated windscreen was specified, in which case the button for that feature occupied the old hazards slot. Later in the Ka's life the heated 'screen control was moved to the other side of the steering wheel and the one-time hazard light hole was once again filled with a blank on all models. The old hazard warning light button itself, however, got to ride again, making a re-appearance in 2000 on the dashboard of the all-new Transit.

The B7-shape Audi RS4 wasn't known for being a featherweight but its creators put some serious effort into shedding kilos where they could. That's why the car had aluminium front wings and bonnet, lightweight sports seats (these alone saving 18kg) and optional carbon ceramic brakes (taking off another five kilos when specced). In order to shave off a total of 50 kilos the engineers also had to bin some bits of equipment such as side airbags and rear electric windows from their flagship, even though many lesser A4s had them as standard. Clearly this was a diet effort too far for the UK and US importers because RS4s sold in those countries didn't have the wind-up windows in the back.

The last Talbot-badged vehicle in production was the UK-only Express van which lasted until 1994. The last Talbot-badged car died seven years earlier when the Horizon went out of production in early 1987.

When the late Ferdinand Piëch was running Volkswagen he decreed that the company's logo should not be overused on its cars and restricted its appearances to the grille and bootlid. Piëch retired in 2002 and, hey presto, the mk5 Golf of 2003 arrived with little VW badges within its headlights. This has carried on to the present day where we have the Golf 8 with the word 'Volkswagen' embossed on its B-pillars. Dr. Piëch must be spinning in his well-engineered grave.

The 1991 Vauxhall Frontera was a re-badged, UK-built version of a Japanese 4x4 called the Isuzu MU. The MU bit of the name stood for 'Mysterious Utility' and in its early life the five-door version was called the MU Wizard. Yes, the Mysterious Utility Wizard. Of course.

Since the 1970s Swedish magazine Teknikens Varld has subjected cars to an extreme swerve through a chicane of cones which it calls the älgtestet or moose test. To this day, the fastest car through the test is the 1999 Citroën Xantia Activa V6 which stayed under control at a max speed of 85km/h thanks to its active anti-roll suspension. Surprisingly, the second placed car at the time of writing is a Nissan Qashqai tested in 2019 which passed the test at 84km/h, 1km/h faster than the third placed Audi R8 V10. The slowest car ever tested is the Reliant Rialto which could only manage 43km/h and almost toppled over.

When Porsche upgraded the 924 to the 924S in 1986 it didn't just fit a 'proper' Porsche engine, a 148bhp version of the 2.5-litre four-cylinder from the 944 in place of the VW EA831 2-litre used in the Audi 100 and Volkswagen LT van. It also gave the new model five stud hubs where the original 924 had only four.

The world's largest car factory by size is Volkswagen's Wolfsburg plant which covers a chunky 6.5 million square metres. In terms of output, however, VW's mothership is beaten by Hyundai's Ulsan plant in South Korea which has an annual capacity of 1.6 million cars. Wolfsburg can manage only around half that every year, hitting a record 836,000 cars in 2014.

Up until his death in June 2020 legendary Porsche engine maestro Hans Mezger drove a car with one of his brilliant motors in it but not some immaculate 996 Turbo or 997 GT3. No, his personal car was a slightly scruffy 1977 911 Carrera 3.0 in Grand Prix White.

The BMW iX3 EV arrived in German showrooms in January 2021 and was on sale for just seven months before it received a major facelift in August of the same year. This isn't the shortest time a derivative has been sold before awkwardly clattering into a significant refresh for the model on which it was based. The V8-powered MG ZT 260 went on sale in September 2003 only for a facelift of the entire ZT range to arrive just four months later in January 2004.

Peter Horbury, the man credited with re-inventing Volvo design, says that when a first generation S80 drives past he "can't look at it" because he now thinks the back end is "maybe half an inch wider than it should be".

Lots of cars with automatic gearboxes have a winter mode but the GT variant of the mk5 VW Golf fitted with the supercharged AND turbocharged 1.4 TSI engine was unusual in having a winter mode for the manual gearbox option too. It limited torque in lower gears to make driving easier in slippery conditions.

Between 1980 and '82 Subaru offered American-market versions of its GL 4WD wagon and hatchback and the BRAT pick-up with a third, central headlight concealed behind the grille badge. Billed by Subaru as the 'passing light' or 'center light', the extra lamp was operated by a separate dashboard switch which would cause the badge to flip out of the way and the light to turn on, though for what reason it's not entirely clear.

Despite being powered exclusively by petrol-fuelled V8s, the mid-engined Corvette C8 has a diesel glow plug warning light hidden within its dash. This is not because General Motors is considering a diesel-powered Corvette in future but because the warning lamp panels flanking the digital instruments, though exclusive to the 'Vette, were subject to GM's 'standardization process' so that the same parts could be used in other models if necessary. Since that might include vehicles with diesel derivatives the glow plug lamp was included to be on the safe side. Nonetheless, when questioned about why the Corvette has this redundant symbol on its dash a GM spokesman hastily insisted, "We plan to remove the icon in the future".

If you're trying to work out whether a Jaguar XE is powered by petrol or diesel and it hasn't got any badges, look at the exhausts. Diesels have a pair of pipes sitting next to each other on the left side of the car, on petrols it's two pipes but one at each end of the central bumper valence. Sadly this identification technique only works on the higher powered models. On lower powered variants the tailpipes are completely hidden, whatever the fuel.

The only UK-market original-style Mini ever fitted with the 1100cc version of the A-series engine was the

1100 Special of 1979, built to mark 20 years of Mini production. The square-nosed Mini Clubman did have the 1100 engine in the UK from 1975 until it ended production in 1980 and Minis made in BMC/BL plants in Belgium and Australia offered the 1100 engine as a regular production model long before Brits got their 1100 special edition. Incidentally, to British eyes the 1100 Special might have seemed full of lavish, model-specific touches such as a unique two-spoke 'sports' steering wheel, new wheel arch extensions and side repeaters on the front wings but unbeknownst to most UK buyers these items were already fitted to some Euro Minis. The cost-effective makeover clearly worked; BL intended to sell just 2500 examples of the 1100 Special but ended up building 5100 cars in order to meet demand.

The wheelbase of the current VW Polo is about the same as that of the mk2 Passat.
(Alright Captain Picky, there's two millimetres in it.)

The styling of the 2022 Nissan Z contains various references to its forebears, the most obscure of which is the design of the nose which is said to be inspired by the 1971 240ZG, a homologation special created to qualify the 240Z for racing in the FIA's Group 4 category for 'grand touring cars'. The G in the name stands for 'grand'. The ZG featured an extended fibreglass 'aero-dyna' nose with fared-in headlights as well as wheel arch extensions rivetted to its sides and a rear spoiler, plus a standard five-speed gearbox and limited slip diff. The 240ZG was sold only in Japan though its extended beak, referred to as the 'G-nose', was available as a dealer-supplied accessory in the US, thereby allowing it to be fitted to 240Zs competing in SCCA races.

The first president of the SAAB Owners' Club of Great Britain was a professional wrestler. Jackie Pallo, who used to fight with legends such as Big Daddy and Giant Haystacks in the seventies, was a serial SAAB buyer who believed he and his son owed their lives to the strength of a 96 they were in which rolled over on the M6 as they returned from a contest in Lancashire. In the nineties Pallo told writer Simon Garfield "I have lots of SAABs", many reportedly rotting in the undergrowth of his garden in Kent. Jackie Pallo died in 2006 during General Motors' disastrous stewardship of his beloved car company although, as far as anyone knows, the two things are not related.

Alfa Romeo's Alfasud project included the construction of a brand-new factory in which to make the car, located in Pomigliano d'Arco near Naples in southern Italy, the idea being to bring greater employment to the region. However, this wasn't new territory for Alfa since Pomigliano d'Arco was already the home of their aviation division which had operated a factory there since the 1940s. The new car plant, opened in 1972, was built next door. The aero factory still exists, though Alfa has long since sold its aviation division which, after merging with FiatAvio, is now part of General Electric under the name Avio Aero. At the time of writing the car factory, now known as the Giambattista Vico Plant, makes the Fiat Panda.

The groovy Opel GT of 1968 and the Vauxhall/Opel Calibra of 1989 were styled by the same man. Before his death in 2020 at the age of 92, designer Erhard Schnell said of all the cars he worked on, the Calibra was his favourite.

The Pontiac Solstice was not a very successful car but the project had a happy outcome for the exterior and interior designers because they later married. Franz von Holzhausen came up with the sketches that were selected for the exterior style while Vicki Vlachakis created the interior theme and the pair worked closely together to see the car to its production debut in 2005. They didn't marry until some years later, however, by which time the Solstice had been cancelled and the entire Pontiac brand killed off. Franz von Holzhausen is now chief designer at Tesla while Vicki von Holzhausen, née Vlachakis, has left the car industry to establish a vegan leather bag and accessories company called von Holzhausen.

When BMW launched the new Mini in 2001 an unusual number of the publicity photos featured models standing in close proximity to the car. This was done deliberately to give a sense of scale, without which the Mini marketeers worried the car's cartoonish looks gave potential buyers a false idea of its size.

Peugeot stopped selling cars in the United States in 1991 yet it kept an office in Little Falls, New Jersey well into the 2000s, complete with a fleet of specially imported current models for employees to use. This led to regular perplexed internet posts from Americans who had spotted, say, a 406 or 307 driving down the New Jersey Turnpike. The office was ostensibly to maintain spares support for owners of old Peugeots in the US, though it's not clear how many people worked there or indeed when it was officially closed down. However, if you call the office today you get a warning that the number is currently not in use. Bad news if you need an alternator for your Federal-spec 505 GL.

The design of the third generation Renault Mégane and the livery and interior of the Eurostar e320 train were overseen by the same man. Fabio Filippini was Design Director for the X85 project which became the 2008 Mégane and Scenic before leaving Renault in 2011 to join design house Pininfarina which had the job of designing the Eurostar specific parts to create the e320, based on the Siemens Velaro.

Peugeot made just 1046 examples of the 405 T16 saloon - a turbocharged, 200 horsepower version of the 405 Mi16x4 - 10 of which went to Les Brigades Rapides d'Intervention, the motorway patrol unit of the Gendarmerie. You could identify these BRI cars by their cloth seats, where regular T16s had leather and Alcantara upholstery.

The Hyundai Veloster has a weird, asymmetric door layout which puts a single, longer door on one side and a pair of doors on the other. The design is 'handed' so that the longer door is always on the driver's side whether the car is right- or left-hand-drive and in theory this means that Hyundai could make a three-door version, or a five-door, just by combining the bodyside stampings in the right combinations. However, they are apparently so wedded to this model's lopsided USP that no such experimentation has ever taken place.

The Audi A2 had five stud hubs, except for the economy-minded 'three-litre' A2 1.2 TDI which featured just four per wheel.

Even after Ford's ill-fated Premier Automotive Group broke up in the 2000s, Volvo continued to test its cars on the interesting British roads shown to its engineers by colleagues at former Group-mates Jaguar and Land Rover. Hence it was sometimes possible to encounter Swedish-registered Volvos on the lanes of Warwickshire and why, in 2013, a bizarrely mutated XC70 – most like a mule for the second generation XC90 – was papped by a Car magazine reader in Wetherby, West Yorkshire.

The first prototype of the four-seat Lamborghini Espada had massive gullwing doors, just like the Marzal concept car which inspired its design. The doors were dropped for production, possibly because they wouldn't have met US regulations of the time (or maybe just because Ferruccio Lamborghini disliked them) and the gullwing prototype was left to rot in the boneyard at the back of the Sant'Agata Bolognese factory (as immortalised in a photo story in the June 1987 issue of Car magazine). The car was later rescued and restored and now lives safely in the Lamborghini factory museum.

First published in 1895, Autocar is one of the world's longest-running magazines but there have been unscheduled gaps in its weekly publication routine. Notably, in 1926 The General Strike caused The Autocar to disappear from newsstands for three weeks. A second major hiatus came in November 1973 when strikes, the energy crisis and the three-day week forced the mag to pause publication. In this instance Britain was starved of car news and road tests for over four months until Autocar returned in March 1974.

Nine out of ten Daimler DS420 limousines were ordered in black.

VOLKSWAGEN GROUP ENGINES FROM
THE PEAK PIËCH ERA THAT HAD
WEIRDLY LIMITED USE
AND/OR LIFESPAN

3999cc W8
Used only in the VW Passat W8 (2001-2004)

5934cc V12 TDI
Used only in the Audi Q7 V12 TDI (2008-2012)

1191cc 3-cyl TDI
Used only in the Audi A2 1.2 TDI (2001-2005) and
VW Lupo 3L TDI (1999-2005)

ENGINE ORIENTATIONS OF SUCCESSIVE GENERATIONS OF VW PASSAT

Mk1 - Longitudinal
Mk2 - Longitudinal
Mk3 - Transverse
Mk4 - Longitudinal
Mk5 - Transverse
Mk6 - Transverse

The re-born Ford Bronco and the latest Land Rover Defender have nothing in common, save that they're both modern evocations of classic models from their respective manufacturers but they could have been closely related. At the turn of the century Ford hatched project U260, a scheme to make a new Bronco based on the chassis of the Ranger pick-up, while in the early 2000s Ford-owned Land Rover investigated the possibility of making a new Defender, also based on the Ranger (as mentioned in the first boring car trivia book). The Land Rover project floundered because all the sums said it couldn't turn a profit while in Detroit U260 died because, ironically, Ford needed to tighten its belt after spending big on Land Rover (and Jaguar and Volvo, and the Firestone tyre recall). Incidentally, Ford still has a U260 styling model from 2001 and in August 2021 dug it out to display alongside the new Bronco production model at the Hagerty Concours d'Elegance of America car show in Michigan.

In the late 1970s the South Korean government sought to rationalise the country's over-capacity motor industry, aiming to whittle it down to a single car-making company. To that end, it gave Hyundai the choice of specialising in cars or power generation equipment, fully expecting that its bosses would plump for the latter, and was surprised when instead they went for cars. It's a decision that seems to be working out okay for them.

Algeria was the last country in which you could still buy leaded petrol for cars. In July 2021 the Algerians finally exhausted their stockpile of leaded petrol, marking the moment at which the world's car fleet finally became lead-free. The UN estimates that finally banishing lead from automotive fuel will prevent 1.2m premature deaths globally and save $2.44 trillion a year not only in health costs but also thanks to lower crime as lead in petrol has been linked to heightened criminal activity.

Endurance testing for the bespoke 205/70 VR15 Dunlop SP Super tyre fitted to the Jaguar XJ-S was carried out on the Jabbeke autoroute in Belgium where the company had set speed records with the XK120 in the 1940s and '50s.

When the Chrysler UK design team showed off the finished clay model for what would become the Alpine its fashionable, angular style met with objections on two fronts. The first came from France, where Chrysler Europe manufacturing engineers said the very flat panels would be impossible to make. The second came from the USA, where head office insisted the company had certain standards for the curvaceousness of metalwork which this proposal did not meet. Design boss Roy Axe dealt with the first problem by buying an equally un-curvy Audi 80 which he parked next to the Alpine clay when the head of manufacturing came over to visit, allowing him to casually observe that the Germans could achieve something the French apparently found impossible. This cunning reverse psychology got the head of manufacturing on side and he was happy to send over two of his people to meet a man from Detroit who arrived in the UK armed with designers' curves to illustrate where this new model went wrong. The two Frenchman listened to the American's objections, shouted some rude things at him (in French) and let him return to the US after which they simply ignored his objections and saw the car through to production in all its angular glory.

The original codename for the first Lexus LS was F1, standing for 'Flagship 1'.

The Clubsport version of the Porsche 968 showed such devotion to weight saving that engineers didn't stop at the usual deletion of back seat, electric windows, central locking and remote mirrors. They also binned the heated washer jets, under-bonnet light, and even the exterior lock for the tailgate which was filled in with a crude plastic blanking plug.

At the launch of the Coupé Fiat the head of the company's Centro Stile, Nevio di Giusto, said the car's unusual headlight covers were designed to look like "a drop of water under the influence of wind". The designer of the Coupé, Chris Bangle, had a different take, however. He said they looked like "a bum".

Every new Aston Martin V12 Vanquish came with a day-long performance driving course which didn't just address how to get the most out of the car at speed. It also featured instruction on how to drive at low speed, essentially coaching owners not to creep along in stop-start traffic as they would in a normal auto because this would burn out the clutch on the much-maligned automated manual gearbox. Obviously, one way to avoid having to give owners lessons in leaving big gaps in traffic jams would have been to offer the car with a conventional clutch pedal and gear stick but Bob Dover, Aston's chairman at the time, insisted that the company's flagship must seem high-tech, hence the paddle shift. In 2006 Aston's Works Service division came to the rescue, however, by offering an aftermarket full manual conversion, initially priced at £13,250 plus VAT.

If you opened the side-hinged tailgate of any Toyota RAV4 from the first three generations to a full 90 degrees the boot-mounted spare wheel would obscure one of the rear light clusters, breaching a UK requirement which says both rear lights must be visible even when the boot is open. To get around this, Toyota fitted British RAV4s with a shorter tailgate checkstrap which restricted opening to rather less than 90 degrees, to the chagrin of owners trying to get large objects into the boot. Many got around the problem by retrofitting the longer check strap fitted to Japanese and US-market models.

In 1998 GM introduced the right-hand-drive Cadillac Seville STS to the UK and picked 12 dealers from Vauxhall's vast network to sell it. They didn't have much luck. In 1999, the car's first full year on sale, just 127 found homes and you can safely assume many of those homes were the ones occupied by Vauxhall management and the dealer principals at those 12 Cadillac outlets. Sales success continued to elude the V8-powered saloon until in early 2002 GM cut its losses and withdrew the car from Britain. For a long time afterwards six unregistered Sevilles could be seen languishing in a compound next to Vauxhall's Luton factory, clearly visible to traffic passing on the way to nearby Luton Airport. That is until the owner of a local cab firm spotted these orphans and marched straight round to Vauxhall HQ where he demanded to see a fleet sales representative. A deal was struck to sell him all six unloved cars for a bargain price and that's how one of Cadillac's brief attempts to sell its cars to Britons ended at the minicab rank.

In official Porsche code, the right-hand-drive version of the 944 is actually the 945.

CELEBRITIES WHO HAVE OWNED A LOTUS CARLTON

Jasper Carrott

CELEBRITIES WHO HAVE OWNED A MERCEDES-BENZ SLR McLAREN

Donald Trump
Jay Leno
Kanye West
Michael Jordan
Paris Hilton
Pharrell Williams
Prince Naseem Hamed
Swizz Beatz
Thierry Henry

The transmission in the McLaren F1 was made by FF Developments, the same people who created the ground-breaking four-wheel-drive system in the 1966 Jensen FF.

In 1989 Peugeot introduced a special edition of the 205 hatchback and cabriolet called the Roland Garros which had quite a tennis-y flavour, what with its green paintwork, part white(ish) leather seats and, on the cabrio, a white hood, plus brochures and ads that featured tennis balls and trophies and depicted the model parked on a clay court. Many buyers, especially outside of France, might not have realised that Roland Garros himself wasn't a professional tennis player and was, in fact, a pioneering aviator. However, he gave his name to a Parisian sporting venue, Stade Roland Garros, and this in turn resulted in the official name of the French open tennis tournament which was held there, Les Internationaux de France de Roland-Garros, hence the tennis theme of these specials. This limited edition 205 clearly worked well for Peugeot because its later replicated it across many other models in its range though M. Garros himself wasn't around to enjoy this as he was fatally shot down in 1918.

Today Subaru is forever associated with four-wheel-drive cars but its relationship with AWD only started because a Japanese regional electricity company was looking for new work vehicles that gave some of the ability of their previous trad 4x4s while offering car-like comfort. As part of this quest, in 1969 a representative from Tohoku Electric Power Company contacted a Subaru dealer in Miyagi Prefecture and asked if it would be possible to convert the company's front-wheel-drive Subaru 1000 estate car to all-wheel-drive. The dealer obliged, modifying eight of the light van versions of the estate for the power company using a Datsun rear axle and diff to achieve its aim. The conversion was such a success that the dealership showed its prototype to Subaru head office which thought it was a tremendous idea and the rest is history. The first factory-built AWD Subarus went on sale in 1971.

Gilbern might be the only car company co-founded by a butcher. Giles Smith was the village butcher in Church Village near Pontypridd when he teamed up with German-born engineer Bernard Friese to build a one-off special which the pair put together in the old abattoir behind Smith's shop. This machine was such a success that in 1959 they formally started a car company, using the first few letters of their respective names to Christen it, and completed their first customer cars in that old abattoir before moving to a proper factory in 1961. Gilbern went out of business in 1973 but Smith's old butcher's shop still stands, though it's now a branch of Lloyds Bank so don't go in asking for lamb chops.

Skoda intended to sell just 300 Felicia Funs in the UK. However, it underestimated the British appetite for a bright yellow hatchback-based pick-up with a pair of slide-out back seats that had no roof over them and in the end 612 right-hand-drive Funs were made in order to meet demand.

When it was launched in 1975 the Rolls-Royce Camargue was the most expensive production car in the world with a list price of £29,250, just £400 less than the cost of TWO Silver Shadows.

In the late eighties Land Rover embarked on a round of improvements for the Range Rover under the title 'CONSTEEL', the first part denoting the CONcealed front door hinges which arrived in 1990, the latter referring to the STEEL boot floor phased in for 1991 models. As part of this project engineers re-checked the dimensions of the Range Rover using the latest measuring methods and belatedly discovered that some fit and finish issues might have been because the shell was longer on one side than the other.

In 2004 Smart announced plans to make a Merc GLK-based SUV called the ForMore and issued a sketch of the car with a Michigan licence plate reading VAC810N, giving away that this was the first Smart created specifically with America in mind. A concept version of the car was built, to be shown off at the following Frankfurt Show ahead of the real car going on sale in 2006 but if you visited that motor show in September 2005 you won't have seen it because a few months earlier the entire ForMore project had been abruptly cancelled. The completed concept car was shoved into a Mercedes storage warehouse while running prototypes of the showroom car were fed into a crusher so hastily that they still had their canvas camouflage panels attached.

In 1974 Chrysler started pushing its upscale Imperial Lebaron line by boasting about seats available in optional 'Corinthian leather'. Then, the following year, the company got actor Ricardo Montelbán to advertise its new Cordoba coupé with a television advert in which he purred about seats upholstered in "soft Corinthian leather" and the phrase really took off. These Chryslers must be pretty fancy, people might have thought, what with this Corinthian leather they have. Except there's no such thing as Corinthian leather. It was a term rather brilliantly invented by copywriters at Bozell, Chrysler's advertising agency. Corinthian leather wasn't actually anything special, it came from a factory in Newark, New Jersey where Chrysler sourced a lot of its leather. Clearly the made-up label worked, however, because Chrysler was still using it, and getting Ricardo Montelbán to say it very elegantly in TV ads, up until the end of the eighties.

Volvo was determined that the original XC90 would avoid the aggressive mannishness of most SUVs and to this end assembled a California-based all-female focus group to steer the car's design. The group included Swedish actress Maud Adams, best known as the eponymous lead in the 1983 Bond film Octopussy, though she also played Scaramanga's mistress in The Man With The Golden Gun and, for the really eagle eyed, appeared in the back of shot as an extra in A View To A Kill. It's not clear if it was this hattrick of Bond films that got her the XC90 job though.

One the stand-out features of the R129 Mercedes SL when it was launched in 1989 was a concealed roll bar which would pop up to protect the occupants in various sub-optimal situations including, of course, a roll over. A switch on the dash also allowed the bar to be gently raised and lowered at will but the hydraulics that allowed this wouldn't have been fast enough to deploy in an emergency so when the car detected an accident an electro-magnetic solenoid instantly disconnected the hydraulics, allowing the roll bar to be briskly flipped upwards by springs normally held under tension by that same hydraulic system when the bar was down.

SPECIAL EDITIONS VOLKSWAGEN MADE IN ASSOCIATION WITH BANDS IN THE 1990s

Golf Pink Floyd
Golf Rolling Stones Collection
Golf Bon Jovi Edition

SPECIAL EDITIONS CREATED WITH FASHION LABELS

Austin Metro Principles
Bugatti Veyron Fbg par Hermès
Chrysler 300C John Varvatos
Fiat 500 by Gucci
Fiat 500 DIESEL
Fiat Panda Trussardi
Ford Explorer Eddie Bauer*
Ford Fiesta Dash
Lamborghini Murciélago LP640 Versace
Maserati Quattroporte Ermenegildo Zegna
Peugeot 205 Lacoste
Rover Paul Smith Mini
SEAT Mii by Mango
Subaru Forester L.L.Bean
Subaru Outback L.L.Bean

*There have also been Eddie Bauer editions of the Aerostar, Bronco, Excursion, Expedition, F-150 and Taurus X.

Four-wheel-drive Audis of the 1980s had a dashboard button to switch off the ABS. The reason for this has its roots in Audi's original quattro four-wheel-drive system, first seen on the Quattro of 1980, which allowed the driver to lock the centre and rear diffs. However, when ABS was introduced it was incompatible with diff locking since it required a difference in wheel speed to operate and locked diffs don't allow this. Instead, the ABS automatically disengaged when the differentials were locked and Audi capitalised on this function by allowing the driver to turn off the anti-lock brakes at other times too, boasting in adverts that on gravel and uncompacted snow it was actually better to let the wheels lock and build up a 'wedge' in front of the tyre to help stop the car. This might have been true, but as the quattro system (and ABS brakes) became more sophisticated such driver intervention became less important and in the early nineties the Audi ABS override button was quietly dropped.

Although it was commonly said that the Coupé Fiat was based on the Tipo, technically it was actually based on the Tipo-derived Alfa 155, a later evolution of the platform which featured, amongst other things, longer front wishbones for a wider track. The Coupé also featured modified bulkheads, to the benefit of its styling, and a shell that was three times stiffer than that of a Tipo.

The Jensen FF was only made in right-hand-drive. Packaging the car's radical four-wheel-drive system involved mounting the engine off to one side, leaving no room for a left-hand-drive steering column and plans to remedy this with some kind of contrived belt system came to nothing.

When the Mercedes-Benz CLS Shooting Brake was launched in 2012 buyers could spend an extra £4030 to have the boot floor lined with cherry wood.

Car makers routinely disguise their prototype and pre-production cars to avoid giving rivals and the media too much of an idea about what they've got coming up and to ensure they get a big splash out of the official reveal. Unfortunately, even modern 'swirly wrap' camouflage can get in the way of snagging work on things like wind noise which is why during development of the fifth generation Range Rover engineers snuck a completely undisguised prototype of the car out of the lesser-known back gate at their Gaydon R&D centre in the dead of night and took it for a nocturnal run around the lanes of Warwickshire to investigate an issue that the camo was impeding. To make sure the top-secret car wasn't revealed so far ahead of its launch, it was preceded at all times by an anonymous current production car containing Land Rover staff on the lookout for anything that might require it to stop or slow down, exposing it to the risk of being papped by some keen-eyed night owl.

The rear wing on the US-spec Jaguar Project 7 was mounted slightly further forward than on cars built for the rest of the world due to American rear impact rules. As a result, Project 7s sold in the USA generated slightly less downforce.

Aston Martin has gone bust seven times.

REFERENCES
A few of the publications and websites referred to
while compiling this book

A Life In Style by Roy Axe
AROnline
Autocar
Car
Car & Driver
Car Guys vs Bean Counters: The Battle For The Soul Of American Business by Bob Lutz
Citroënet
evo
Fast Forward: Confessions of a Post Punk Percussionist: Volume II by Stephen Morris
Jalopnik
Range Rover First Generation – The Complete Story by James Taylor
The Real R3 Story by John Batchelor and Craig Cheetham
The Road Rat
Secret Fords by Steve Saxty

THANKING YOUS

Tom Barnard, Robert Brink, Ant Brown, Craig Cheetham, Ian Elliott, Louis Gardner, Alex Goy, Ollie Horsley, John Lakey, Bryan McMorran, David Pook, Jonny Smith, Peter Stevens, Andy Wheel

WISE COUNSEL
Keith WR Jones

COVER DESIGN
Russell Wallis

COVER CARS

Aston Martin DB3S - front grille
Audi A3 (8L) - rear light
Audi A3 (8Y) - lower air intake
BMW 3 Series (E36 coupe) - side windows
BMW Z3 - side vent
Corvette C3 - bumper and lower grilles
Hummer H3 - front grille
Jaguar XJ series 3 - rear lights
Land Rover Series III – headlight, sidelight and indicator
Mazda3 - front grille
Mazda MX-3 - headlight, indicator and fog light
MG3 - back door
Morgan 3 Wheeler - rear
SAAB 9-3 - rear lights
Tesla Model 3 - wheel
Triumph TR3 - front grille
Volkswagen Type 3 - side grilles

ABOUT THE AUTHOR

Richard Porter is the founder of sniffpetrol.com, the former script editor of Top Gear and The Grand Tour, a columnist for evo magazine, a contributor to The Road Rat and The Sunday Times, a writer of scripts for various TV shows and one half of Smith and Sniff, the UK's number one automotive podcast. Boring Car Trivia 3 is his third volume of boring car trivia, although you probably knew that thanks to a subtle clue in the title.

Printed in Great Britain
by Amazon

76810327R00066